PricewaterhouseCoopers Guide to Charitable Giving

Michael B. Kennedy, MBA, CPA, PFS

Evelyn M. Capassakis, JD, LLM

Richard S. Wagman, JD

JOHN WILEY & SONS, INC.

Published by John Wiley & Sons, Inc., Hoboken, New Jersey
Published simultaneously in Canada

For general information on our other products and services, or technical support, please contact our Customer Care Department within the United States at 800-762-2974, outside the
United States at 317-572-3993 or fax 317-572-4002.

Wiley also publishes its books in a variety of electronic formats. Some content that appears in
print may not be available in electronic books.

Library of Congress Cataloging-in-Publication Data:

PricewaterhouseCoopers guide to charitable giving / by PricewaterhouseCoopers.
    p. cm.
Includes index.
    ISBN 0-471-23503-2 (paper : alk. paper)
 1. Income tax deductions for charitable contributions—United States.
I. Title: Guide to charitable giving.   II. PricewaterhouseCoopers LLP.
    KF6388 .P75 2002
    361.7'4'0973—dc21

                                          2002005590

Printed in the United States of America

10 9 8 7 6 5 4 3 2 1

Table of Contents

Acknowledgments

Effective tax planning and charitable giving have much in common, with one major difference: when you transfer assets for the benefit of your family members, you seek maximum tax benefit for your family; when you transfer assets for charitable causes, you seek maximum benefit for others. What is best for you based on your needs and desires? Determining your philanthropic goals is the first step in developing an effective charitable giving strategy to support your intentions.

This book represents the accumulated knowledge and experience of PricewaterhouseCoopers' (PwC) Personal Financial Services professionals who, on a daily basis, work with clients, both locally and globally, in addressing their charitable intentions, developing strategies that allow them to realize their charitable and non-charitable goals.

In particular, we would like to thank William R. Fleming, Director in PwC's Hartford office, Christine M. Lamprecht, Manager in our Philadelphia office, David D. Green, Partner in our Los Angeles office, and Andrew C. Martone, Senior Manager in New York City for their outstanding contributions toward making this book a success.

We also express gratitude to the many partners and professionals of PwC who have significant experience in developing wealth transfer strategies designed to fulfill personal goals and support charitable causes.

Michael B. Kennedy
Partner, National Director of Personal Financial Services

Evelyn M. Capassakis
Partner, Personal Financial Services

Richard S. Wagman
Partner, Personal Financial Services

Chapter 1
Introduction

Private philanthropy has long been a cornerstone of financial support for charitable organizations in the United States. In addition to the obvious benefits to society, philanthropic support provides the donor with a tax-efficient means to transfer wealth.

The tragic events of September 11, 2001, created a substantial surge in charitable contributions intended for victims of the disasters and their families. Scores of new organizations were created to collect contributions and disburse funds to the intended recipients. The IRS acted rapidly to expedite the process for organizations to apply for exempt status.

Although the primary motive of charitable giving to an organization is to support a charitable purpose, tax planning plays an important role. In recent years, the IRS has increased its scrutiny of charitable giving. For example, substantiation requirements for income tax deductions have been made more stringent and the use of charitable trusts has been limited.

The basic tax rules on charitable giving revolve around when the donation takes place, whether the recipient is a "charity," what gifts qualify, what substantiation is needed, what the amount of the deduction is, and what limitations apply.

To benefit from a gift of a charitable contribution, a donor must itemize deductions on his or her tax return. There was a brief time when charitable deductions were permitted without the need to itemize deductions and eliminating the need to itemize is a recurring tax proposal. For higher income taxpayers, itemized deductions are subject to a reduction based on income; this adjustment is also scheduled to change.

Donors to charities are faced with many options. For example, an individual may wish to transfer assets outright to a charity or retain an interest for a period of years so that an income stream is created for the donor or named beneficiaries. By understanding the basic rules and working with a tax professional, donors can benefit themselves, family members, or other individuals and the charitable organizations of their choice.

This book explores different charitable giving alternatives, focusing on current gifts, deferred or planned gifts, gifts of income and annuities, and charitable bequests. It covers the advantages and disadvantages of each type of gift, as well as the funding alternatives and assets that may be utilized. Finally, the book describes the federal tax implications of charitable giving. Federal tax aspects include income tax, estate tax, and gift tax aspects of different charitable gifts. State tax law treatment of charitable contributions should also be reviewed when considering charitable contribution planning.

The rules relating to gifts by corporations, trusts, and estates, however, are generally beyond the scope of this analysis. In addition, the tax rules applicable to transfers to non–U.S. charities are not discussed in any detail.

These charitable giving strategies have been developed from the combined experience of many professionals at PricewaterhouseCoopers. The recommended tax planning techniques should be useful in a wide variety of situations, but they may not be appropriate for everyone. Because each individual has unique circumstances, a tax professional should be consulted before implementing these strategies.

Chapter 2

September 11–Related Charitable Contributions

Following the September 11 terrorist attacks many new charitable organizations sprung up, accepting contributions to aid victims and their families. The IRS cooperated by creating an expedited procedure for the new organizations to apply for exempt status by using IRS Form 1023, Application for Recognition of Exemption Under 501(c)(3) of the Internal Revenue Code, and writing "Disaster Relief, Sept. 11, 2001" at the top of the form. The IRS even established a toll-free number for exempt-organizations determinations: (877) 829-5500.

To assist taxpayers who wish to contribute to organizations formed specifically to assist victims of the September 11 attacks, the IRS posted a list of the newly formed organizations that have been granted tax-exempt status on its web site (www.irs.gov). Contributions to these organizations are tax-deductible. The IRS has begun to review its determinations and has kept the list updated. Of course, pre-existing charitable organizations, to which contributions are deductible, may also be providing September 11–related disaster relief assistance.

IRS also has released on its web site a copy of a new publication entitled "Disaster Relief: Providing Assistance Through Charitable Organizations." The full text of this publication appears in Appendix D of this book.

Employer-Sponsored Leave-Sharing Donation Programs

In the aftermath of the September 11, 2001 terrorist attacks, a number of employers have adopted or are considering adopting leave-based donation programs, under which employees forgo vacation, sick, or personal leave in exchange for employer contributions to charitable organizations. The IRS has issued interim guidance (Notice 2001-69, 2001-47 IRB) on the tax treatment of these programs and the proper reporting of payments by employers.

The IRS's position is that employees aren't subject to payroll or income tax on vacation time, sick leave, or personal leave that they give up in exchange for their employers' contributions to charitable organizations. Employees are not entitled to a charitable contribution deduction for these forgone amounts. For their part, employers may deduct these donations as business expenses, which aren't subject to the limitations that apply to charitable contributions. The interim guidance applies to employer contributions made before 2003.

Chapter 3

Types of Charitable Organizations

The Internal Revenue Code states that a charitable contribution is either a contribution or gift to certain enumerated organizations (generally known as Sec. 501(c)(3) organizations) which are organized and operated exclusively for religious, charitable, scientific, literary, or educational purposes, or is a contribution or gift to governmental units or entities for a public purpose. Each year, the IRS issues a list of qualified charitable donees in Publication 78, "Cumulative List of Organizations Described in Section 170(c) of the Internal Revenue Code."

A portion of the IRS web site (www.irs.gov) lists qualified charitable organizations. From the IRS web site, type "Publication 78" in the search box and you will be directed to the online version of IRS Publication 78, the list of qualified charitable organizations. The organizations listed by the IRS have generally obtained an exemption letter from the IRS that verifies their tax-exempt or "Sec. 501(c)(3)" status. Certain charitable organizations, such as churches or smaller charities, however, need not obtain an exemption letter from the IRS.

Public Charities

A public charity is a tax-exempt organization that is organized and operated exclusively for religious, charitable, scientific, literary, or educational purposes and either receives broad public support or is a church, school, hospital, or organization operated to support another public charity. Public charities are also known as Section 501(c)(3) and Section 170(c) organizations.

Well-known and popular charitable organizations are typically public charities.

Private Foundations

A private foundation is a tax-exempt organization that is organized and operated exclusively for religious, charitable, scientific, literary, or educational purposes *but does not* meet the broad public support requirements that would classify it as a public charity. Private foundations are also considered Section 501(c)(3) organizations.

An individual or family often establishes a private foundation. In addition, many corporations establish foundations in their names.

The major difference between public charities and private foundations is the limitations on deductions. Another important difference is that most private foundations are subject to an excise tax on investment income each year.

Observation

It should be noted that the IRS has stepped up its review of private foundations to ensure that no inappropriate acts of "self-dealing" between donors and their private foundations exist. Private foundation managers and contributors must be especially careful of any transactions involving the private foundation.

There are two types of foundations—operating foundations and non-operating foundations.

Operating and Non-operating Foundations

Most private foundations do not actively conduct their own charitable activities and are classified as "non-operating." Operating foundations actively conduct charitable activities.

Non-operating foundations are required to make distributions equal to at least 5% of the fair market value of their assets each year. The charitable contribution deduction for an individual to a non-operating foundation generally is limited to 30% of the individual's adjusted gross income (AGI) for gifts of cash and 20% for gifts of appreciated property such as stock. Non-operating foundations are also subject to an excise tax on their investment income (including capital gains) each year.

Operating foundations are those that actively conduct a program of charitable activities, rather than merely provide passive support to other charities. Individuals can claim a charitable deduction of up to 50% of AGI for contributions to these entities—the same as for contributions to public charities. Operating foundations are usually organizations such as museums, libraries, or care facilities for the elderly.

A **pass-through private foundation** is a private foundation that distributes all of its annual gifts plus its investment income in any given year. In this case, the higher 50% AGI limit on charitable contributions applies. (see Chapter 7). The decision to make distributions and achieve pass-through status can be changed from year to year.

Community Foundations

A community foundation is a public charity that is designed to attract assets for the benefit of a particular geographic area. Community foundations are treated as public charities (not as private foundations), so the donor has a large degree of flexibility both in structuring the gift and in advising the foundation on how to benefit the surrounding community. Because a community foundation is a public charity, it is not subject to excise taxes.

Donor-Advised Funds

A donor-advised fund is a specially segregated donation to a public charity. The fund is distributed based on the donor's wishes. The donor does not have

any legal right to compel specific uses for the donated funds, but most charities feel a moral obligation to follow the donor's wishes. Many mutual fund
families, large banks, and many community foundations have established
donor advised funds.

Donor-advised funds are an alternative to establishing a private foundation
while avoiding the record-keeping, filing, and other administrative chores
associated with private foundations. Further, the funds generally can be
established with smaller amounts than would be needed to justify the
expense of maintaining a private foundation. Finally, donor-advised funds are
not subject to the annual excise tax on investment income.

Observation
Donor-advised funds have become a popular way to contribute to
charitable organizations and maintain a continuing active role in
how the contributions are used.

Supporting Organizations

A supporting organization is a privately organized, donor-influenced (but
not controlled) organization that supports a named public charity. In many
respects it is similar to a private foundation. The major difference is that the
board of a supporting organization must be linked to that of the public charity it supports.

The supporting organization is treated as a public charity for purposes of the
contribution deduction and reduction rules (see Chapter 7). Further, the supporting organization is not subject to an excise tax on investment income.

For example, supporting organizations can be created with collectibles (art,
antiques, historic automobiles, historic boats, and so forth) that are loaned
out on a periodic basis to public charities. This permits a variety of charities
to benefit from a particular collectible item.

Chapter 4

Deductible and Non-deductible Contributions

In order for a contribution to qualify for a charitable deduction, there must be a gift. A gift is generally defined as a transfer of something of value with no consideration given or expected in return. Thus, if there are "strings" attached to a donation, it may not qualify as a gift.

At one time, donative intent was an important element of a charitable contribution. The courts and the IRS looked for such factors as lack of consideration expected or received (*i.e.,* lack of "quid pro quo") and for "detached and disinterested generosity." Today, the issue has narrowed to whether any "quid pro quo" benefits have been received by the donor and the value of those benefits.

Contributions of money or property generally are deductible if given to:
- Churches, synagogues, temples, mosques, and other religious organizations
- Federal, state, and local governments if made solely for public purposes (for example, a gift to reduce the public debt)
- Non-profit schools and hospitals
- Public parks and recreation facilities
- Salvation Army, Red Cross, CARE, Goodwill Industries, United Way, Boy Scouts, Girl Scouts, Boys and Girls Clubs of America, among others
- War veterans' groups

In addition, charitable deductions may be taken for expenses paid for a student sponsored by a qualifying organization living with the donor, and out-of-pocket expenses paid by a donor who serves a qualified organization as a volunteer if certain conditions are met.

Contributions are NOT deductible if made to:
- Political action committees
- Social and sports clubs
- Chambers of commerce
- Trade associations
- Labor unions
- Certain social welfare organizations
- Most foreign charities
- Political parties
- Organizations that engage primarily in lobbying activities
- Other non-qualified organizations

In addition, payments made for tuition; raffle, bingo, or lottery tickets; and dues, fees, or bills paid to country clubs, lodges, fraternal orders, or similar groups, as well as the value of a donor's time or services or value of blood given to a blood bank are all not deductible as charitable contributions.

Payments for Schooling

There have been attempts made to deduct payments made for children's education. Such payments made to colleges and universities or to church-affiliated schools for education are not deductible. The substantiation requirements, detailed in Chapter 6, should make it clear when deductible contributions versus non-deductible payments for services have been made.

Fund Raising Events

Charitable organizations often hold special events for donor groups or to encourage additional contributions. These fund raising activities include lunches, dinners, formal banquets, concerts, golf tournaments, or shows. The substantiation requirements (see Chapter 6) now require that the charity provide the donor with a statement as to the deductible and non-deductible portions of any tickets or admission charges.

Of particular concern are games of chance such as raffles, bingo, or number matching. Amounts paid to participate in such activities are not deductible at all.

Membership Dues and Fees

Many charitable organizations charge fees or dues to use their facilities (e.g., rent church hall for wedding reception). Normally, fees and dues are not deductible unless the amount charged is in excess of the value received. Charities are now required to provide donors with information about the deductible portion of the payment.

Token Benefits

Charities sometimes provide low-cost giveaway items to promote the charity's name. Giveaway items are not part of the deductible versus non-deductible calculation as long as the value of the item is small. The IRS has extensive guidance on this area for charitable organizations.

Athletic Event Preferred Seating

Many colleges and universities offer programs that allow donors to accumulate points or credits toward preferred seating arrangements. Members of such programs are permitted to purchase desirable seats for athletic events. After years of court battles over what value to assign to such special seating opportunities, Congress created an arbitrary standard.

Only 80% of a "contribution" made to a college or university is treated as a charitable contribution if the contribution entitles the donor to preferred seating arrangements. The remaining 20% is non-deductible.

Use of Vacation Home or Other Property

The gift of a temporary right to use property does not give rise to a charitable contribution deduction. The contribution of the use of a vacation home (or the sale of a week's use of a vacation home at a charitable auction) is not deductible. In fact, such use of the vacation home is treated as personal use (which may have other income tax effects). Further, allowing a charity to use office space rent-free does not create a charitable deduction.

On the other hand, donating an undivided interest in a property does create a charitable contribution deduction. The undivided interest must be a percentage of the total.

Non–U.S. Organizations

In order to qualify as a charitable contribution, the recipient organization must be a domestic organization. Thus, a contribution to an organization that is not based in the United States will not qualify for an income tax charitable deduction. In fact, if the donor contributes appreciated property to a foreign trust, the donor may incur income tax on the gain. Donors considering foreign charities should investigate whether the organization has a U.S. affiliate that would qualify as a charitable organization for U.S. tax purposes.

Note that U.S. organizations are permitted to carry on charitable activities in countries other than the United States and still have contributions to the organization qualify for a charitable deduction. They are, however, regulated by and subject to U.S. tax rules.

Chapter 5

When Deductible

A charitable deduction will be allowed only after the rights of actual possession in the donated property shift from the donor (and those parties related to the donor) to a qualified charitable organization. In addition, special rules pertain to gifts of tangible personal property (related to the recipient organization).

A contribution is considered made when delivery occurs. There are a variety of ways the time of delivery is determined.

Gifts by Check

Gifts by check are deductible when the donor loses control of the check. A check is presumed delivered when it is put in the mail and clears the donor's account in due course. A check mailed near year-end is deductible in the year mailed even if the charity cashes the check in the next year.

Gifts of Securities

Gifts of securities are deductible when there has been unconditional delivery of the stock certificate. Depending upon how the certificate is transferred, there are a variety of considerations. Since security values vary day by day, the method chosen to transfer the property will influence the deductible amount.

If the stock certificate is properly endorsed and mailed, then delivery (and the contribution deduction) takes place at mailing as long as the charity receives the certificate in due course. Note that the certificate must be properly endorsed for this rule to apply.

The delivery of a stock certificate to the donor's broker for transfer does not result in delivery until the transfer has been recorded on the books of the corporation. Instructing a broker to transfer shares in street name to a charity does not result in a charitable contribution until the transfer is recorded on the books of the corporation or until the shares in street name are in the hands of the charity's broker or brokerage account.

The preferred method of transferring securities is for the charity to name the broker as an agent (by creating an account) and having the broker acknowledge the agency in writing. Then contribution takes place when the brokerage firm records the transfer on its books.

Note that securities nearing an income recognition event (liquidation or taxable takeover) must be transferred before the event is finalized to avoid having the income taxable to the donor.

Example

Donna has stock in Widget, Inc., which is being acquired in a cash transaction by another company. She wants to donate her Widget stock to charity rather than pay capital gain tax on the takeover payment. She doesn't want to make the donation until she is sure that the transaction is "certain." After shareholder vote and stock tendering is nearly complete, she gives the stock to her college. She is entitled to a charitable contribution for the stock but is also subject to income tax on the gain. She waited too long to contribute the stock.

If the securities are donated with an "understanding" (such as an agreement for a transaction) between the donor and the charity then the charitable donation deduction might be at risk. This is often the case with closely held stock: the donor will transfer the stock and the company will redeem the shares soon after the transfer. As long as the "understanding" is not legally binding in any way (not put rights, call rights, or pre-existing sale arrangements), the IRS will not treat the redemption as a dividend to the shareholder/donor.

Observation

In an extreme example, one court case deals with a donor who contributed a significant amount of stock to a charity with the understanding that the charity would then purchase a yacht from the donor (the donor no longer wanted the yacht and was having trouble selling it). The donor was treated as if he had sold the stock and donated the yacht.

Credit Card Gifts

Many organizations accept credit card gifts. A contribution charged to a bank credit card is deductible by the donor in the year the charge is made.

Pledges and Notes

A pledge is nothing more than a promise to make a gift. Until the pledge is satisfied by cash, check, or other means, no charitable contribution deduction is allowed. Likewise, issuing a promissory note as payment of a charitable contribution is not deductible as a charitable contribution until the note is satisfied.

Real Estate

A gift of real estate is effective for charitable deduction purposes when a properly executed deed to the property is delivered to the charity. Note that the recording of the deed (important to protect property rights) is not the triggering date.

Options

Granting or transferring options to a charity does not create a deduction at the time of transfer. Instead, the deduction is triggered at the time the charity exercises the option. The amount of the deduction is based on the market value of the property compared to the option price. Further, if an employee transfers stock options to a charity, the exercise of the option triggers compensation income to the employee even though the charity owns the option at exercise. For this reason, employee stock options are not considered a useful tool in charitable giving.

Chapter 6

Substantiation

A recent battleground in charitable contributions is substantiation. Any charitable contribution less than $250 can be substantiated by check. A charitable contribution of $250 or more must be substantiated in writing by the charity (the cancelled check is NOT sufficient).

Written acknowledgement (such as a thank-you note) from the charity is now critical for a valid charitable deduction.

The substantiation requirements also force a charitable organization that provides goods or services in excess of $75 to a donor in exchange for a contribution to furnish to the donor a written statement of the deductible amount and a good faith estimate of the value of the goods or services provided.

Gifts Less Than $250

Gifts of less than $250 (calculated on a gift-by-gift basis) can be substantiated by check. Because the calculation is done on a gift-by-gift basis, a series of $249 gifts will not be combined in order to apply the more strict substantiation rule described below. Payroll deduction gifts fall in this category.

Gifts Greater Than $250

Single gifts of $250 or more *cannot* be substantiated by check. Instead the IRS requires that the donor have a statement from the charity that provides certain required information. The statement from the charity must be received before the donor files his or her tax return.

The charity's statement must contain *all* of the following:

    The donor's name

    A description of the property contributed

    The date of the contribution

    The amount or value of goods and services received by the donor (if any)

    The fact that no goods or services were received by the donor (if none)

    The name and address of the donee organization

If a donor does not have a statement from the charity, the deduction is disallowed. The donor is permitted to request a "proper" statement as long as he or she receives it prior to the due date of the return (including extensions) or the date the return is filed (if earlier).

Chapter 7

Reductions and Limitations

Sales of certain appreciated property held for longer than one year will produce long-term capital gains. A contribution of this type of property to certain charities usually generates a deduction equal to the fair market value of the donated property. The advantage of a contribution is that it avoids recognition of gain and the resulting tax. This provides an obvious incentive for a donor to contribute appreciated long-term capital property to a charity rather than sell the property and donate the proceeds.

> ***Observation***
>
> The opposite applies to property that has declined in value. It generally would be more beneficial to sell the property first and recognize any potential loss, and then donate the cash proceeds to charity.

Example

Donor has publicly traded stock worth $75,000 with a cost basis of $25,000. If the donor sells the stock, she will recognize $50,000 of capital gain and pay $12,500 of capital gain tax (average 25% combined federal and state rate). Donor nets $62,500 of funds to donate and receives a charitable deduction for $62,500. If, as a preferred alternative, donor instead donates $75,000 stock directly to charity, donor recognizes NO gain and receives a $75,000 charitable contribution deduction.

Charitable Contribution Reduction

There are several very specific situations where the amount of the charitable contribution deduction is reduced when appreciated property is donated. These rules are designed to avoid potential abuse.

The contribution deduction is reduced for *ordinary income property* donations. Ordinary income property is defined as property that would produce ordinary income if sold by the donor. The contribution deduction is the fair market value of the property less the amount of ordinary income not recognized. Ordinary income property includes business inventory, works of art created by the donor, letters and memoranda written by the donor, and life insurance policies.

This same reduction rule applies to capital gain property that has been held for one year or less, that is, property that would produce short-term capital gain if sold. *Short-term capital gain property* includes recently acquired stocks, bonds, real estate, or collectibles.

The reduction rule also applies to contributions of *tangible personal property* if the property is not related to the exempt function of the charitable organization receiving the property. Tangible personal property includes such things as art, antiques, and jewelry.

> **Example**
>
> Donor gives a valuable painting to an art museum. The painting will be displayed in the museum along with other works. The tangible personal property item (art) is related to the function of the museum and the contribution deduction is *not* subject to the reduction rule. If donor gave the painting to a food bank, the contribution deduction would be reduced.

The reduction rule also applies to gifts of *long-term capital gain property to a private foundation*. Note that there is a significant exception for "qualified appreciated stock," that is, publicly traded stock. The exception for "qualified appreciated stock" applies for gifts of publicly traded stock of which family members own not more than 10% of the total. Thus, gifts to a private foundation of closely held stock are subject to this reduction rule while gifts of publicly traded stock are *not* subject to the reduction rule (see Chapter 3 for a description of the types of private foundations).

Percentage Limitations

After determining that a transfer of property is a contribution eligible for a charitable deduction, a donor often is surprised to find out that the Internal Revenue Code places limits on the annual deduction. These limitations are based on an individual's annual contribution base, generally equal to the individual's adjusted gross income (AGI). The limitations depend on the character of the charitable organization (public charity versus private foundation) and the type of property (cash versus long-term capital gain property). The percentage limitation rules are very complex and the following material is simply a brief discussion. Donations in excess of the annual limitations can be carried forward. The carryover of charitable contributions is limited to 5 years.

The limitation for cash contributions is 50% for gifts to public charities (and operating foundations) and 30% for gifts to private foundations. Thus, if a donor's charitable contributions are greater than 50% of his AGI, the excess is carried over.

Table 7.1 *Percentage Limitations*

Type of Gift	Deductible Amount	AGI Limitation	
		Public Charity(1)	Private Foundation (PF)
Cash	Fair market value	50%	30%
Ordinary Income Property Such As: • Inventory • Short-term Capital Gain Property • Depreciable Property	Lesser of fair market value or adjusted basis	50%	30%
Appreciated long-term capital gain property	Fair market value except: • certain contributions to a PF—limited to adjusted basis • personal property not related to tax-exempt purpose—limited to adjusted basis	30%(2) or 50%	20%
Publicly Traded Stock	Fair market value	30%	20%
Carryover		5 years	5 years

(1) Private operating and pass-through private foundations are subject to the same AGI limitations as public charities.

(2) Donor can elect to apply the 50%-of-AGI limitation by decreasing the deductible amount for any potential long-term capital gain. Election applies to all gifts given that year.

These percentage limitations apply to contributions made directly "to" charities. Lower percentage limitations may apply to contributions made "for the use of" charities (such as contributions to some trusts).

For estate purposes, there are no limitations on the deduction available to a decedent's estate. All contributions made by bequest are deductible based on the property's full fair market value.

Example

John's adjusted gross income is $75,000. His maximum charitable contribution for cash gifts is $37,500 if made to a public charity and $22,500 if made to a private foundation.

The limitation for capital gain property donations is 30% for gifts to public charities (and operating foundations) and 20% for gifts to private foundations. If a donor's charitable contributions are greater than 30% of her AGI, the excess is carried over.

Example

Jane's adjusted gross income is $100,000. Her maximum charitable contribution for appreciated publicly traded stock is $30,000 for public charities and $20,000 for private foundations.

These limitations are for income tax purposes only. Different and less restrictive rules apply to bequests.

Corporations

The annual limit for charitable contribution deductions by corporations is the same whether or not the contributions are made to private foundations, private operating foundations, or public charities so long as the contribution is used only in the United States or its possessions for charitable purposes. Essentially, the limit is 10% of taxable income after certain adjustments, with a 5-year carryover.

Chapter 8

Valuation and Appraisals

A donation that qualifies as a charitable contribution must be valued in order to determine the deductible amount. Valuation is the responsibility of the donor who is claiming the charitable contribution deduction. Proper valuation is doubly important because undervaluing a contribution will reduce the available charitable deduction and overvaluing could subject the donor to additional taxes, interest, and penalties.

For contributions of cash, value simply equals the dollar amount donated.

For contributions of property, valuation becomes more difficult. IRS regulations state that charitable contributions of property, other than money, will be valued at "fair market value" at the time of the contribution, subject to certain reductions discussed later. "Fair market value" is defined as "the price at which the property would change hands between a willing buyer and a willing seller, neither being under any compulsion to buy or sell." Encumbrances or debts on such property will also affect the value of the contribution and the tax consequences to the donor.

Charitable Contribution Valuation

In determining fair market value of donated property, one or more of four different factors are most often used. They are *opinions of experts, cost or selling price, sales of comparable properties*, and *replacement cost*. See

25

Table 8.1 for questions you should consider when using these factors for valuing property contributed to a charitable organization (according to the IRS).

Table 8.1 *Determining Fair Market Value*	
When using this factor:	**Questions to consider:**
Opinions of experts (aka Appraisals)	Is the expert knowledgeable and competent?
	Does the written opinion state the purpose for the valuation?
	Is the written opinion thorough and supported by facts and experience?
Cost or selling price	Was the purchase or sale of the property reasonably close to the date of contribution?
	Was any increase or decrease in value, as compared to actual cost, at a reasonable rate?
	Do the terms of purchase or sale limit what can be done with the property?
	Was there an arm's length offer to buy the property close to the contribution date?
Sales of comparable properties	How similar is the property sold to the property donated?
	How close is the date of sale to the contribution date?
	Was the sale at arm's length?
	What was the condition of the market at the time of sale?
Replacement cost	What would it cost to replace the donated property?
	Is there a reasonable relationship between replacement cost and fair market value?
	Is the supply of the donated property more or less than the demand for it?

Listed below are valuation guidelines for different types of assets. Note that sometimes contribution reductions must be taken into account.

Asset	Valuation Guidelines
Cash	Dollar amount
Tangible property	Retail price
Traded stocks and bonds	Exchange price (average of high and low)
Closely held businesses	Appraised value (could be subject to "discounting")
Life insurance	Interpolated terminal reserve or replacement cost
Real estate	Appraised value
Artwork	Appraised value (or cost if donated by artist)

The following describes the valuation rules for several types of property that are commonly contributed to charity.

Property Available to the Public at Retail

The value of the charitable contribution for property sold to the public is generally the retail price at which the property would be sold (there are some exceptions for dealers or businesses). For example, a passenger van donated by an individual to a charitable organization to be used by that organization to fulfill its charitable purposes would be valued at the price at which the van would sell to the general public, rather than to an automobile dealer.

Observation

Donations of property in excess of $5,000 require both an appraisal and completion of Form 8283 (see Appendix C).

Traded Stocks and Bonds

Contributions of stocks and bonds are valued at the fair market value of the stock or bond as of the date of the gift. For stocks and bonds traded on a stock exchange or other public market where values can be easily ascertained, the fair market value is the average between the highest and lowest selling prices on the date of the contribution. If the stock or bond was not traded on the date of contribution but was traded within a reasonable period of time before and after that date, the donor would use a weighted average of the highest and lowest selling prices before and after the date of contribution. If the stock or bond was not traded within a reasonable amount of time, the fair market value is determined by averaging the *bona fide* bid and ask prices on the date of the contribution or by using the weighted average system discussed above.

> **Observation**
>
> Traded stocks and bonds do not require an appraisal, even if the donation is in excess of $5,000.

Interests in Closely Held Businesses

Contributions of interests in a closely held business pose particularly difficult valuation problems. An outside appraisal by a qualified appraiser is advisable to determine the fair market value for contribution purposes. The IRS indicates that a "willing buyer/willing seller" analysis should be used to determine value, and provides that the following additional factors should be considered:

- A fair appraisal as of the date of the contribution of all tangible and intangible (including goodwill) assets of the business;
- The demonstrated earning capacity of the business; and
- The dividend-paying capacity, the economic outlook of the industry, the company's position in the industry, the degree of control of the business represented by the block of stock to be valued, and the value of any other comparable business whose stock is traded on a stock exchange.

Observation

The practice of "discounting" (reducing the value to reflect the lack of control connected with minority interests or lack of marketability of non–publicly traded stock) has become a popular technique to reduce gift or estate tax liability. It is possible that the IRS may apply the concept of discounting the value of a charitable gift to "discount" the value of charitable donations of such stock.

Observation

Charitable gifts of closely held stock will likely receive more IRS scrutiny because of the inherent valuation concerns. Care should be taken to ensure that proper valuation procedures are followed. Donations of interests in non-traded businesses in excess of $10,000 require an appraisal and completion of Form 8283. For gifts of closely held stock not requiring an appraisal, a partial summary of the property is required.

Interests in Notes

The fair market value of any note is calculated by adding the unpaid balance to the interest accrued up to the date of the contribution. The donor may be required to report a different value if there are factors to warrant an alternative valuation. Such factors include interest rate fluctuations, the ability to collect on the note, and the fact that the property pledged as security is insufficient to satisfy the obligation. Note that any uncollected interest is ordinary income property subject to reduction rules (see Chapter 7).

Observation

Donations of interests in notes in excess of $5,000 require an appraisal and completion of Form 8283.

Interests in Life Insurance

The valuation of contributions of life insurance can depend on whether the insurance policy requires additional premium payments in future years. Further, the reduction rules will apply to a life insurance policy (see Chapter 7).

The fair market value of a single premium policy transferred immediately after payment is the cost of the policy. The fair market value of a paid-up insurance policy is the amount that the issuer of the policy would charge for a similar policy of the same specified amount on the life of a person who is the same age as the insured at the time of the contribution.

For contributions of insurance policies with premiums still due, determination of the fair market value is more complex. Typically, the issuing company can assist donors of unpaid insurance policies in determining the fair market value for charitable contribution purposes. Any additional premium payments will result in additional charitable contributions that are deductible in the year paid.

Observation

Donations of life insurance in excess of $5,000 require an appraisal and completion of Form 8283. Further, the deduction may be reduced (see Chapter 7).

Interests in Real Estate

Contributions of real estate also present valuation problems. Competent appraisers are needed to determine the fair market value for charitable contribution purposes. Generally, real estate is appraised using one of three valuation methods or a combination of these methods. Such factors as time of prior sales, location of properties, and interest rates need to be considered in valuing donated real estate. The comparable sale method compares the donated property to other similar properties that have been sold. Other methods of valuation include the capitalization of income method, which incorporates an analysis of the present value of income to be produced in the future, and the replacement cost method, which determines the cost required to replace the donated property.

Contributions of real property subject to a mortgage are deductible only up to the amount of value in excess of the mortgage. A contribution of debt-financed property is deemed a bargain sale, and some capital gain will likely be realized. For more detail, see "Bargain Sales" in Chapter 9.

> **Observation**
>
> Donations of real estate in excess of $5,000 require an appraisal and completion of Form 8283.

Paintings, Antiques, and Other Objects of Art

The IRS is especially troubled by contributions of paintings, antiques, and other objects of art. Contributions in excess of $5,000 require an appraisal and completion of Form 8283. Contributions in excess of $20,000 must be accompanied by a complete copy of the signed appraisal and color photograph of a size and quality that shows the object fully. The IRS uses a special panel of experts to value paintings, antiques, and other objects of art.

For artwork that has been appraised at $50,000 or more, the donor may request a Statement of Value for the item from the IRS.

> **Observation**
>
> The donor must pay a user fee of $2,500 for a Statement of Value for one to three items of art. This fee is not refundable unless the IRS refuses to issue the Statement of Value "in the interest of efficient tax administration."

Jewelry and Gems

As with other property donations, contributions in excess of $5,000 require an appraisal and completion of Form 8283. The appraisal should describe (among other things) the style of the jewelry, the cut and setting of the gem, and whether it is still in fashion. The stone's coloring, weight, cut, brilliance, and flaws should be reported and analyzed.

> *Observation*
>
> Sentimental personal value has no effect on the value of the jewelry. If, however, the jewelry is or was owned by a famous person, its value might increase.

Cars, Boats, and Aircraft

Commercial firms and trade organizations publish periodic guides to dealer sale prices for recent model years of cars and other vehicles. These prices are not "official" for valuing specific donated property, but they do provide clues for making an accurate appraisal of fair market value.

> *Observation*
>
> The IRS has instructed its examiners to look closely at donations of used autos. It is wise to donate only to reputable charities and to not be overly aggressive in valuing your donated auto. Be sure to keep evidence of its condition, such as photos, and maintenance records and receipts.

> *Observation*
>
> Donations of cars, boats, or aircraft in excess of $5,000 require an appraisal and completion of Form 8283.

Used Clothing and Household Goods

The value of both used clothing and household goods is usually much lower than the price paid when new. The price that buyers of used items actually pay in stores selling these goods, such as consignment or thrift shops, is an indication of fair market value. Some organizations provide sample price lists for use by donors. Another alternative is to look over shop merchandise and prices.

Observation

Donations of used clothing and household goods in excess of $5,000 require an appraisal and completion of Form 8283.

Hobby Collections

Collectibles are often the subject of charitable donations. Most common are rare books, stamps, coins, natural history items, manuscripts, autographs, and so forth. Many of the rules applicable to paintings and other objects of art (discussed above) also apply to miscellaneous collections. Collectors' publications or price guides often help determine the value of many types of collections.

Observation

Be certain to use the current edition at the date of contribution of collectibles price guides. These sources are not always reliable indicators of fair market value and, where the collection has significant value, should be accompanied by an appraisal from an expert.

Observation

Donations of collections in excess of $5,000 require an appraisal and completion of Form 8283.

Appraisal Requirements

As discussed above, any charitable deduction claimed in connection with a contribution of property valued in excess of $5,000 ($10,000 for gifts of closely held stock) must be supported by a qualified appraisal. The appraisal must be summarized and attached to the tax return in order to substantiate the deduction.

IRS Form 8283 (printed in Appendix C) has been designed to gather this information; the information required is summarized in the chart that follows. The IRS can disallow a charitable deduction if a required appraisal is not secured. A "qualified appraiser" generally is someone who holds himself or herself out to the public as an appraiser or performs appraisals on a regular basis, and has qualifications to value the particular type of donated property.

The weight given to an appraisal depends on the completeness of the report, the qualifications of the appraiser, and the appraiser's demonstrated knowledge of the donated property. An appraisal must give all the facts on which to base an intelligent judgment of the value of the property.

Observation

The IRS may accept the claimed value of the donated property, based on information or appraisals sent with the return, or make its own determination of fair market value.

Observation

A charitable deduction may not be taken for fees paid for appraisals of donated property. However, these fees may qualify as a miscellaneous deduction (subject to the 2% limit) on Schedule A (Form 1040) if paid to determine the amount allowable as a charitable deduction.

Table 8.2 *Information Reporting Requirements*

Donated Property	Appraisal Required	Non-cash Charitable Contributions Form 8283	Appraisal Attached	Appraisal Summary	Partially Completed Summary	Donee Information Reporting*
Artwork valued over $20,000	X	X	X	X		X
Deduction of $500 or less						
Deduction claimed between $500–$5,000	X	X			X	X
Deduction claimed over $5,000	X	X		X		X
Closely held stock $5,000–$10,000		X			X	X
Closely held stock over $10,000	X	X		X		X

*If sold, exchanged, consumed, or otherwise disposed of within 2 years after receipt of the property, the donee may have to report on Form 8282 (see Appendix B).

As noted earlier, the substantiation rules and IRS enforcement are strict. No deduction is allowed for any contribution in excess of $250 that is not substantiated by the charitable organization (such as a thank-you note). The thank-you note must indicate the amount of the contribution and the value of any goods or services provided to the donor. For single contributions of $250 or more, a canceled check is not considered a valid form of substantiation.

Penalties for Overvaluation

Penalties assessed for overstating the value of a charitable contribution can be quite severe. In order for a penalty to be assessed, the portion of the tax underpayment attributable to the valuation misstatement must exceed $5,000. If the value reported on a donor's tax return is 200% higher than the actual value, the IRS will subject the taxpayer to a penalty equal to 20% of the portion of the underpayment. If the valuation misstatement is deemed "gross" (reported value is 400% greater than the actual value), the penalty is equal to 40% of the underpaid tax.

The Internal Revenue Code provides a reasonable cause exception to this penalty. For valuation misstatements related to charitable contribution property, the donor must prove that the value claimed was based on an appraisal performed by a qualified appraiser and that the donor made a good faith investigation of the value of the donated property.

Chapter 9

Special Interest Current Gifts

Once you have decided to make a charitable contribution, it is important to be aware of all the funding options available. Charitable contributions can be funded with common assets, such as cash, securities, and real estate, as well as with less common assets, such as closely held business interests, notes, accounts receivable, art, collectibles (coins and stamps), books, antiques, jewelry, cars, boats, planes, patents, royalties, contract rights, life insurance, and easements. Almost any asset you own can be donated currently or can fund a deferred giving plan. This chapter discusses several of the more popular assets used for charitable giving.

Although no one rule applies to every charitable contribution, a few ground rules bear repeating. First, the amount of the charitable deduction is usually the fair market value of the donated property. However, if tangible personal property is donated and is not used by the charity for its exempt purpose, the value of the deduction will be reduced to the tax basis of the property.

Second, any debt assumed by the charity on the donated property will result in classifying that transaction as a bargain sale (see "Bargain Sale" discussed in this chapter).

Third, short-term capital gain and ordinary income property are valued at cost rather than fair market value. Therefore, it is more advantageous to donate long-term capital gain property because the donor will receive a deduction for the fair market value of the property rather than its tax basis.

S Corporation Stock

Many individuals who own interests in closely held businesses have elected to benefit from the S corporation rules. The tax rules regulating S corporations allow certain charitable organizations to be permitted S corporation shareholders. Gifts of S corporation stock, like gifts of closely held stock, should be planned carefully to ensure that the best tax results are achieved for both the donor and the charity.

> *Observation*
>
> A further option that should be considered by S corporation owners is a charitable lead trust that is treated as a grantor trust.

Artwork

Works of art are popular assets for funding charitable contributions. Generally, the amount of the charitable contribution is the fair market value of the artwork. However, if the donor is the artist, the contribution is limited to the donor's cost basis. It is also important to note that a donation of artwork must include all copyrights to the artwork in order to qualify for a present deduction (see discussion of copyrights below).

If the donor does not donate the entire interest (or an undivided percentage of the entire interest), the partial interest rules will prevent the donor from receiving any tax deduction. Individuals contemplating a contribution of artwork should consider donating their entire interest or possibly an undivided partial interest in the artwork.

Example

Mr. R owns a painting with a fair market value of $100,000 and a tax basis of $25,000. Mr. R donates an undivided 25% interest in the painting to a qualified charity and currently receives a $25,000 charitable deduction. This donation requires Mr. R to allow the charity to display the painting for 25% of each year, but Mr. R has accomplished four important goals:

1. He provides a benefit to a charity.
2. He receives a $25,000 charitable deduction.
3. He retains enjoyment and possession of the painting for 75% of the year.
4. He can precisely control the current charitable contribution amount by adjusting the percentage donated.

Mr. R's insurance costs also can be partially reduced because the charity assumes the cost of insuring the art while it has the art in its possession.

Partnership Investments

Contributions of interests in partnership investments qualify for charitable deductions. However, problems arise in valuing the interest to determine the deductible contribution amount. Many charities are not interested in receiving partnership interests (especially family limited partnerships or limited liability companies). The charity may refuse to accept the donation if it cannot dispose of the partnership interest quickly and easily.

Generally, the contribution amount is equal to the fair market value of the partnership interest. That amount must be adjusted, however, for the donating partner's share of unrealized receivables and appreciated inventory (ordinary income property). The donating partner must also recognize ordinary income from outstanding installment obligations of the partnership on the date of the contribution.

Any partnership liabilities or non-recourse debt assumed by the charity upon acceptance of the partnership interest as a donation will cause the transaction to be treated as a bargain sale. Under the bargain sale rules, the donor is required to recognize gain on the donation of the partnership interest to the extent the debt assumed exceeds the allocated tax basis.

Oil and Gas Interests

To value a charitable contribution of an oil and gas interest, donors must reduce the fair market value of such interests by the amount of any ordinary income they are entitled to receive on the date of the contribution. This is because oil and gas interests generally produce ordinary income. Oil and gas interests held by the donor for more than one year generally qualify as long-term capital gain assets. Thus, any capital gain on the investment will escape taxation to the donor.

Because of the nature of the oil and gas industry, certain investments in oil and gas properties are treated as mortgages (that is, production payments). Under this treatment, the charity will be viewed as assuming these debts upon receipt of the donation. As for all transactions in which a charity assumes any debt of the donor, the bargain sale rules will be triggered and the donor may recognize a taxable gain on the transaction.

Copyrights

The value of the charitable contribution of a copyright is usually measured by its fair market value on the date of the transfer. Two rules, however, must be considered when calculating the value of the donation: (1) if the donor of the copyright was also the creator of the work to which the copyright applies, the deduction is limited to the donor's cost of creating the copyright; and (2) in the event that the donor owns both the copyright and the work to which it applies, both items must be donated, unless the contribution is made to a pooled income fund, a charitable lead trust, or a charitable remainder trust. If the contribution is not made to one of the above-mentioned deferred-giving vehicles, the donor will not have transferred the entire interest in the asset, and the partial interest rules will prevent the income tax deduction of a current donation by the donor.

Out-of-Pocket Expenses

The tax code permits deduction of out-of-pocket expenses made on behalf of a charity, but prohibits deductions for the value of time or services that may be donated to charitable organizations. Out-of-pocket costs may include volunteer driving, transportation to attend charitable governing functions, charitable related travel, or "hosting" charitable events.

Observation

Unreimbursed expenses you incur as a volunteer, including mileage driven in your car, are deductible. The mileage rate for purposes of the charitable deduction is indexed for inflation and changes from year to year. The 2002 mileage rate is 14 cents per mile.

Many charitable organizations sponsor travel-requiring activities related to their exempt functions. These activities often produce charitable contribution deductions.

Note that in order to be deductible, any charitable related expenses or travel must not produce any significant element of personal pleasure, recreation, or vacation.

Bargain Sales

As discussed above, a bargain sale occurs when a donor sells property to a qualified charity for less than its fair market value or transfers property with debt attached. Such transactions are treated as part sale, part gift. The transaction is divided into two parts.

The first part is the sale of the property to the charity. The second part is the donation to the charity. The donor's cost basis in the asset is divided between the two parts as well.

Example

John has a building worth $100,000 that he bought for $60,000 (there has been no depreciation taken on the building). He would like to donate it to charity, but will need some cash to make some needed improvements to another property. The charity is willing to provide $10,000 to John. John sells the building to the charity for $10,000. His charitable deduction is the market value less the sale price ($100,000 minus $10,000 or $90,000). He also recognizes a capital gain based on the sale price, $10,000, and his basis in the part sold, $6,000. Since he sold 10% of the value, 10% of the basis is assigned to the "sale" portion.

Example

Jane has a building worth $200,000 that she bought for $50,000. Jane has a $100,000 mortgage on the property. She donates it to a local charity. Because the property has a debt, the transaction is part sale and part gift. The gift portion is $100,000 (market value $200,000 less mortgage assumed $100,000). The sale portion is $100,000 (the value of the debt transferred). The gain on sale is $75,000 calculated by dividing the basis between the gift and sale portions.

Life Insurance Gifts

Life insurance is another vehicle for funding charitable contributions. A charity can be named as the beneficiary of a policy. Policy ownership can be transferred to a charity. Finally, life insurance is sometimes combined with deferred giving techniques. Each method has its own benefits and tax consequences.

It is important to note developments at the state level that affect this type of contribution. Several states have statutes prohibiting charitable organizations from owning life insurance policies on a prospective donor. The rationale for such legislation is that the charity does not have an insurable interest in the life of the individual. If the individual purchases the policy and then transfers it to a charity, this problem may be avoided. Before making a contribution of a life insurance policy, donors should review their individual state statutes.

Simply naming a charity as beneficiary of a life insurance policy does not create an immediate income tax charitable contribution deduction. No income tax deduction is available because the policy owner has retained "incidents of ownership"—in particular, the right to change the beneficiary.

The primary benefits of naming the charity as beneficiary are that the individual retains access to the policy's cash value (if needed) and that the individual retains the ability to change the beneficiary. At death, the value of the policy will be included in an individual's gross estate, but it will be offset by an estate tax charitable deduction.

An immediate income tax charitable deduction can be taken only if the owner assigns all interests in the policy to the charitable beneficiary. Any incident of ownership (e.g., the right to change beneficiary, access cash surrender value, or cancel the policy) will prevent the immediate deduction. If all incidents of ownership are transferred, the charitable income tax deduction will be allowed. The amount of the deduction is equal to the cash value of the policy (note that if the cash value is in excess of premiums paid, then the deduction is limited to premiums paid). If there is a policy loan at the time of transfer, the transaction will be considered a *bargain sale* (see prior section in this chapter).

Wealth Replacement Trust

Many individuals are wary of making sizeable donations of cash or property to charitable organizations because of the resulting reduction in assets available to pass on to family members. A method of addressing this concern is to combine the charitable gift with the establishment of a life insurance trust (also known as a wealth replacement trust).

There are two steps involved in this technique. First, the individual makes a charitable gift using a charitable remainder trust pooled income fund or annuity arrangement (discussed in detail in Chapters 10 and 11). Second, the individual establishes a life insurance trust that owns a life insurance policy whose premiums are paid from the tax savings produced by the charitable contribution and the after-tax income from the charitable remainder trust, pooled income fund, or annuity arrangement. The donor's children are named as trust beneficiaries.

If properly structured, the life insurance death benefit will pass to the children upon the donor's death free from estate taxation. By using income tax savings and part of the income received from a charitable remainder trust, one can fund an irrevocable life insurance trust to replace the value of the asset placed in the charitable remainder trust, pooled income fund, or annuity arrangement.

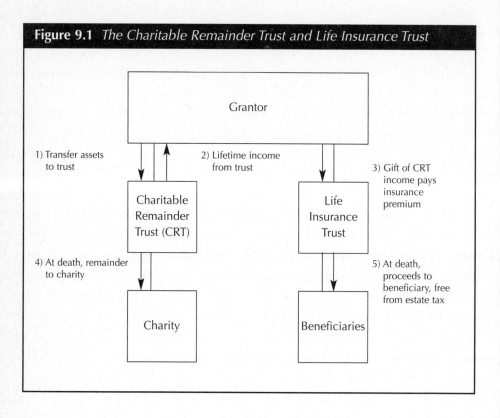

Figure 9.1 *The Charitable Remainder Trust and Life Insurance Trust*

Chapter 10

Deferred Giving and Other Charitable Giving Options

Deferred giving refers to a delayed gift to charity. The most typical deferred gift involves a transfer in exchange for a lifetime benefit. In this case, the charity's receipt of funds is deferred until a future date (the death of the donor).

Deferred gifts to charity can consist of annuity-type arrangements, gifts of the income from property, pooled income funds, and different types of charitable remainder or lead trusts. The flexibility available in being able to match the type of property to the type of charitable gift option is an advantage of this kind of giving. In addition, where neither outright nor deferred giving is possible, there are other possibilities, such as gifts of undivided interests in property, conservation easements, or property restrictions.

Gift Annuity

One of the most popular forms of deferred charitable giving is the charitable gift annuity. In its simplest form, the donor transfers cash, securities, or in some cases real estate to an established charity in exchange for the charity's promise to pay an annuity to the donor and/or other named beneficiaries. The value of the charitable contribution is the difference between the annuity value and the value of the property transferred. In addition, a portion of each annuity payment is deemed a return of the original investment and is tax-free to the annuitant over his or her life expectancy as determined by actuarial tables.

For most charities, rates of return usually are based on tables provided by the American Council on Gift Annuities, an organization originally formed in 1927 as the Committee on Gift Annuities (www.acga-web.org).

The American Council on Gift Annuities has set a recommended rate of return depending on the age of the beneficiary or beneficiaries (gift annuities allow for two beneficiaries). Annuity payments can be designed to be paid out immediately or at some later date (in many cases, annuity arrangements are set up to begin payment at retirement).

Note that the financial stability of the charitable organization is important when considering a charitable gift annuity. The donor receives an unsecured "promise to pay" from the charity and there is no particular asset the donor can look to if the charity experiences financial difficulties.

Pooled Income Funds (PIFs)

A pooled income fund is a trust administered by a charitable organization to which each donor contributes property while retaining an income payment for life. In effect, the pooled income fund acts as a large pooled investment account run much like the charity's investment portfolio.

The property transferred by the donor is commingled with property transferred by other donors. The named beneficiaries receive an income interest determined by the rate of return earned by the trust each year. The only limitation on the trust is that it may not accept or invest in tax-exempt securities.

The amount of charitable deduction allowed is based on the highest investment yield of the fund during the three previous years. In the case of a fund that has been in existence for three years or less, an IRS-set minimum fixed yield (which varies from year to year) must be used to calculate the deduction. Because the charitable donation is of a remainder interest, a higher yield reduces the deduction. The return to the beneficiaries will be treated as ordinary income for income tax purposes. The PIF will provide income tax data to the beneficiary each year for tax preparation purposes.

Example

Mr. W, age 65, owns securities that cost $10,000 and are now worth $50,000. If Mr. W sells the securities, he will pay $8,000 ($40,000 gain × 20%) in capital gains tax, which would leave $42,000 to invest. If Mr. W invests the proceeds and receives a 10% rate of return, he will generate income of $4,200. Alternatively, if Mr. W contributes the securities to a pooled income fund, he will pay no capital gain tax. If the fund pays a similar 10% yield, the $50,000 in securities will produce $5,000 in annual income. Mr. W will also receive a charitable deduction of approximately $14,400, which in a 30% tax bracket saves $4,320 in federal taxes. If the tax savings are invested at the same 10% rate of return, the overall income will be $5,432, a 29% greater income stream than the $4,200 available to Mr. W if he had sold the securities outright.

Remainder Interest

Remainder Interest in a Personal Residence or Farm

The largest asset many individuals own is their personal residence (or farm property). A popular method to avoid estate tax on a personal residence or farm while gaining a lifetime income tax charitable deduction is to give a remainder interest in that property to charity. In addition to the charitable contribution benefits, a gift of a remainder interest in a residence or farm will permit the donor to avoid capital gain tax from a potential sale. The income tax charitable deduction is based on the present value of the charity's remainder interest. Although the personal residence or farm would be included in the decedent's estate, an offsetting charitable deduction is available for estate tax purposes.

The income tax regulations that interpret charitable contributions define a "personal residence" as any property that an individual uses as his personal residence even if not the principal residence (a person's primary home for tax purposes). Thus, a vacation home or a boat can qualify. The term "personal residence" could also include stock owned by an individual as a tenant-stockholder in a cooperative housing corporation if the dwelling the stockholder is entitled to occupy is used as the individual's personal residence. The term "farm" is defined as any land used by an individual for the production of agricultural products or for the sustenance of livestock.

In determining the value of a remainder interest in real property, income tax regulations require that the donor take into account depreciation (using the straight-line method). The regulations point out that the transfer of a personal residence or farm may not be in trust and must be irrevocable.

Undivided Interests

A gift of an undivided interest is an alternative to either outright giving or deferred giving. Distinguishing between a partial interest (no deduction allowed) and an undivided interest (deduction allowed) is difficult. An undivided interest can be summarized simply as a fractional interest.

A gift of an undivided portion of a donor's entire interest must extend for the entire term of the donor's interest in the property. For example, a contribution of the right to display artwork for one month per year would be a partial interest (no deduction allowed), while a donation of a one-twelfth ownership interest in the art would be an undivided interest and would qualify for a deduction.

The following are examples of gifts of undivided interests that qualify for a charitable deduction: (1) an individual owns 100 acres of land and makes a contribution of 50 acres to a charitable organization; (2) an individual who has a life estate in an office building for life makes a contribution of a one-half interest in the life estate; (3) a charitable organization is given the right, as a tenant in common with the donor, to possession and control of a property for a portion of each year.

The transfer of an undivided interest must be complete. If the donor retains some substantial right, the deduction will be disallowed. For example, if the donor gives an interest in historic motion pictures to a charity but retains the sole right to market reproductions, a charitable deduction will not be allowed.

Conservation Easements

A charitable contribution deduction is also allowed in connection with the transfer of a perpetual easement in real property for conservation purposes. The contribution must be made to a qualified organization, generally governmental entities or publicly supported charities. In addition, the property must be used exclusively for conservation purposes: preserving land areas for outdoor recreation by the general public; protecting a relatively natural habitat of fish, wildlife, plants or similar ecosystem; preserving open space (including forests and farms); or preserving a historically important land area or certified historic structure.

For decedents dying after 2000, a qualified conservation easement may be claimed for estate tax purposes with respect to any land that is located in the United States or its possessions.

The value of a contribution of a qualifying conservation easement is the change in fair market value of the property before and after the restriction. Absent comparable sales of easements, the fair market value is determined by comparing the land's fair market value before the restriction is granted to the fair market value after the restriction is granted.

Chapter 11

Charitable Remainder Trusts

Charitable remainder trusts are a popular form of deferred giving. The transfer is accomplished by creating a trust with income paid to individuals and the remainder going to charity. This form of charitable giving allows the donor or other named beneficiaries to receive an income stream from the transferred assets as well as a current charitable deduction. When the trust's term ends, the remaining assets become the outright property of the charitable organization.

> ### Example
> Husband and wife have $50,000 in highly appreciated dividend-paying securities. They wish to make a substantial gift to College G, but are unable to part with the income stream generated by the stock. They can make a deferred gift of the stock to College G, retaining a "life interest" in the income, while creating a "remainder interest" for College G.

A charitable remainder trust is an irrevocable trust created during the life of a donor or by an individual's will. Under the terms of the trust, a specified amount (not less than 5% and not more than 50%) of the trust's net fair market value is paid to one or more beneficiaries (at least one beneficiary must be noncharitable) on an annual or more frequent basis.

Charitable remainder trusts can last for either the lifetime of an individual (or several individuals) or for a period of years (no more than 20 years). A charitable remainder trust requires that the income beneficiaries be alive when the trust is created. The charitable remainder beneficiary may be a private foundation created by the donor. When the non-charitable interests terminate, the remainder must pass to the charity.

There are two main types of charitable remainder trusts: the annuity trust and the unitrust. The charitable remainder annuity trust (CRAT) pays a set dollar amount each year. The set dollar amount is expressed as a percentage of the assets donated to the trust. The charitable remainder unitrust (CRUT) pays a different dollar amount each year. The payout is expressed as a percentage of assets as of the beginning of the year.

A charitable remainder trust generally does not pay income tax on investment earnings (dividends, interest, or capital gain). This permits the trust to sell appreciated property and not trigger gain. The beneficiary of the trust is instead responsible for income tax on amounts received from the trust.

Taxation of Distributions to Income Beneficiaries

The beneficiary of a charitable remainder trust is subject to income tax on the distribution based on a specific set of ordering rules. The ordering rules are based on the amounts and type of earnings within the trust (income baskets). The trust annual information filings track the different baskets of income and order the distributions as follows:

1. Ordinary income (dividends and interest) based on the income earned currently and any amounts not distributed in prior years
2. Short-term capital gains based on the short-term gain in the current year and any amounts not distributed in prior years
3. Long-term capital gains based on the long-term gain in the current year and any amounts not distributed in prior years
4. Tax-exempt income based on the tax-exempt income earned currently and any amounts not distributed in prior years
5. A non-taxable return of capital if all ordinary income, capital gains, and tax-exempt income in the current year and all prior years have been distributed

Observation

These ordering rules make tax-exempt investments a poor economic choice in most cases.

Charitable Contribution Amount

The amount of the charitable deduction is determined by reference to IRS valuation tables and the "Applicable Federal Rate" in order to calculate the present value of the remainder interest. The Applicable Federal Rate (AFR) is published each month (near the end of the prior month) by the IRS and carried in major tax publications. Generally, a charitable remainder annuity trust produces a larger charitable deduction if the AFR is greater. The charitable remainder unitrust calculation is not as affected from month to month.

Actual calculations are based on the rate for the month when the transaction is completed by reference to the "best" rate for the three-month period ending with the current month. The other variables in the calculation are the percentage income interest retained and the duration of the trust (life or term of years). Retaining a greater income interest creates a smaller charitable deduction.

A major requirement is that the charitable deduction must be equal to at least 10% of the value of the property transferred to the trust. Thus, a charitable remainder trust payout must be engineered to produce the desired benefits within the IRS restrictions.

Charitable Remainder Annuity Trust (CRAT)

The charitable remainder annuity trust requires that a "sum certain" figure be paid at least annually to the named income beneficiary or beneficiaries. No additional contributions may be made to the trust over its term and the periodic payment must remain constant (a function of the original contribution amount).

This payment remains the same dollar amount despite changes in interest rates or the performance of the trust's investments (either an increase or decrease in the value of the trust assets). The annuity amount is established at the time the trust is created and affects the charitable deduction. The higher the retained annuity, the lower the value of the charity's remainder interest and, hence, the lower the available charitable deduction.

The IRS has taken the position that no charitable deduction is allowable for a contribution to a CRAT if there is a greater than 5% probability that a non-charitable beneficiary will survive the depletion of the trust property. As a practical matter, this means that either the lifetime income beneficiary must be aged 55 or older or the annuity percentage chosen must equal to or less than the AFR for valuation.

Example

Sam has waterfront property that was purchased for $45,000. He has received several unsolicited offers for the property and the property taxes have increased dramatically. He would like to convert this property into a steady income stream and eliminate the property tax liability, but he does not want to pay a large capital gain tax in the year of sale.

Sam creates a charitable remainder annuity trust for 20 years and retains a 7% annuity. The remainder goes to the general fund of his favorite university. The land is valued at $145,000 by a professional appraiser and is transferred to the trust. The trustees of the charitable remainder trust immediately sell the property for $145,000 and invest the proceeds in CDs that produce $9,500 of interest income each year. Sam will receive an annuity payment of $10,500 per year for 20 years.

Sam will receive an income tax charitable deduction of $45,346 in the year of the transfer (using an AFR of 8%). The sale with $100,000 of gain triggers no current income tax and is recorded in the capital gains "basket" of income for determining the taxability of future annuity payments. The income ordering rules will result in $9,500 of each annual payment being treated as interest income and the remaining $1,000 being treated as capital gain (until the capital gain basket is exhausted).

Charitable Remainder Unitrust (CRUT)

The charitable remainder unitrust is similar to the annuity trust in many respects. The primary difference is in the calculation of the required annual payout to the income beneficiary (or beneficiaries). The unitrust requires annual or more frequent payments to the income beneficiary based on a fixed percentage of the net fair market value of the trust assets valued *each year*. Thus, a CRUT payout will not be the same from year to year (unless the net fair market value of the trust assets remains exactly the same each year). Additionally, a charitable remainder unitrust may receive additional contributions, an option unavailable with the annuity trust. As a practical matter, the payment redetermination each year is much simpler if easy-to-value assets are used.

Because a charitable remainder unitrust provides the donor or other income beneficiary with an annual income stream that is based on a fixed percentage of the trust assets in the year of the payout, this type of charitable remainder trust is more attractive during periods of inflation or if funded with appreciating assets. A donor whose investment policy is geared toward growth over a period of time would also find this option attractive.

Example

Wendy is 75. She owns stock worth $100,000, which was purchased 20 years ago for $20,000. She wishes to diversify her holdings but is unwilling to pay a large capital gain tax.

Wendy places the property into a unitrust. The property is sold by the trust. The trust pays no income or capital gain tax on the sale. The trust pays Wendy 10% of the trust's net fair market value annually for her life. Wendy names her favorite art museum as the remainder beneficiary. The unitrust arrangement provides Wendy with a $41,119 charitable deduction in the year of creation. Because the annual distribution is keyed to the fair market value of that trust each year, she enjoys the benefits (or detriments) of the trust investments if they increase (or decrease in value) from year to year. Wendy's first annual payment amount would be $10,000.

A charitable remainder unitrust is also extremely flexible. It can be structured to pay out the lesser of the trust's annual income or a fixed percentage of the annual value of the trust assets. This type of CRUT is known as a net income only unitrust and can be combined with a makeup provision—net income with makeup (NIMCRUT)—to account for "lean" income years.

Income-Only Unitrust

An alternative to the standard CRUT is the net income–only unitrust. The net income trust distributes the *lesser* of a fixed percentage of the annual value of trust assets or the net annual income of the trust. Another potential feature of the net income–only unitrust is the allowance for a makeup provision. In years where the net income exceeds the fixed percentage, the trust may permit greater distributions to "make up" for lesser distributions in prior years. Net income is often defined as dividends and interest less expenses. Net income does not usually include capital gains (short term or long term). The definition of net income may vary from state to state and is subject to some uncertainty if nonconventional investments are used (partnerships or limited liability companies).

Due to its flexibility, the net income unitrust with make up features (NIM-CRUT) is an ideal asset accumulation vehicle that can be used for meeting specific goals (like retirement planning). An individual can transfer appreciated assets to a NIMCRUT. The trustee can sell the assets without triggering capital gain tax and re-invest in growth assets that produce little or no dividends or interest. The income-only provision requires the trustee to pay out only dividends and interest. Capital growth is not taxed until reinvested in something producing dividends or interest. This allows the trust assets to grow untaxed for a period of time. At some future date, the trustee can rearrange the trust investments and invest in high-income assets. The high-income assets create net income for distribution to the beneficiary.

Example

John places $100,000 of appreciated stock ripe for sale in a NIM-CRUT. The annual unitrust amount is 5% of the trust assets or the net income, whichever is lower. The trust sells the stock and invests in different stocks that do not pay significant dividends (or in zero coupon bonds). The trust earns about $100 of dividends each year (the net income) and pays John $100 each year. John pays tax on the $100 each year. The trust investments grow each year. John retires 10 years later when the trust is worth $215,000. The trustee converts the assets into high income–producing investments. The net income is now $17,200 per year. John will receive both the current 5% unitrust amount, $10,750, and a makeup amount each year until the prior "missed" payments are exhausted.

Charitable Remainder Trusts: Summary of Benefits

- The donor receives a current income tax deduction and an income stream either for life (or lifetimes) or for a term of years (up to 20).
- The donor can contribute highly appreciated assets that can then be sold by the trust without triggering capital gain tax. Likewise, the trust may sell other assets from time to time free from capital gain tax.
- The donor pays income tax on trust payments based on a tiered income system.
- The earnings on the trust assets are usually free from tax.
- The donor can select the rate of return desired when the trust is created.
- A donor can convert low-income property into a higher income stream.

Unrelated Business Income (UBIT)

Charitable remainder trusts cannot be involved in any investments that produce "business income." Business income can come from debt-financed property or business ventures operated as partnerships or limited liability companies. The trustee of a charitable remainder trust must be alert to investments that produce UBIT, or significant adverse income tax results will be triggered.

When to Use CRAT, CRUT, or PIF

CRAT—Converts an appreciated asset into a fixed income stream that is unaffected by fluctuations in trust asset values.

- For individuals with steady income requirements
- Assets can be sold and investments structured to provide tax-advantaged income stream
- No additional contributions allowed
- Simple to administer because annual valuation of assets not required

CRUT—Converts an appreciated asset into an income stream that reflects the fluctuation in value of the assets.

- For younger beneficiaries concerned that inflation will erode value of income stream

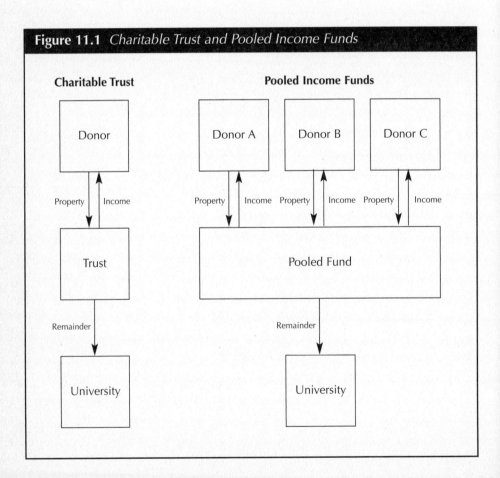

Figure 11.1 *Charitable Trust and Pooled Income Funds*

- Flexible, with income-only and makeup options (excellent for retirement planning)
- Additional contributions allowed
- Hard-to-value assets create practical calculation difficulties
- Not subject to "5% probability rule," so higher payout rates are available

PIF—Generally requires transfer of liquid assets and provides an income stream for life.

- Payout to donor is based on actual income earned
- Charity maintains the fund, so transaction costs are minimal
- Tax-exempt investments are not allowed, so payments are generally fully taxable as ordinary income

Chapter 12

Charitable Lead Trusts

Charitable lead trusts provide that the charity receives the income for a period of years and the remainder goes to a family member or non-charitable beneficiary. A charitable lead trust is the opposite of a charitable remainder trust (see the discussion in Chapter 11). There are two types of charitable lead trusts: the charitable lead annuity trust (CLAT) and the charitable lead unitrust (CLUT).

Upon creation of a charitable lead trust, the donor is entitled to an income tax charitable deduction if the charitable interest is in the form of a fixed percentage of trust assets or a guaranteed annuity *and* if the donor will be taxed on the trust's annual income as it is earned (i.e., a grantor trust). The tax liability can be mitigated if the trustee invests in tax-exempt securities. If the donor establishes a "nongrantor" charitable lead trust, he or she will not receive a charitable income tax deduction, but will not be taxed on the trust's income each year either.

Care should be taken if the charitable organization receiving the income interest is a private foundation established by the same person setting up the charitable lead trust (for lifetime lead trusts). The IRS has ruled that control of the private foundation by the donor means that the gift to the charitable lead trust is "incomplete."

Important gift tax and estate planning objectives can be achieved through the use of a charitable lead trust. The transfer of the property to a family member at the end of the period will result in a current gift for gift tax purposes or trigger estate taxes at death. The gift or estate tax is reduced with a charitable lead trust because the value of the gift is reduced by the value of the income interest given to the charity. The value of the remainder interest passing to family members can be engineered to produce significant transfer tax savings.

The estate tax rules must be taken into account if the "grantor" lead trust option is chosen (the donor gets a deduction but is taxed on the income each year). Certain administrative powers are often used to obtain classification as a grantor trust for income tax purposes. The powers must be carefully chosen or limited, or the assets of the charitable lead trust will be included in the donor's estate (a tax disaster). It is essential to consult with a tax professional before creating a grantor lead trust.

Charitable Lead Annuity Trust (CLAT)

A charitable lead annuity trust pays a set annual amount (expressed as a percentage of the original contribution) to a charity. The actual dollar amount will not change from year to year. There is no minimum or maximum payout percentage required. If the income from the trust is not sufficient to make the payment, then the principal of the trust must be paid out. A charitable lead annuity trust's investments must be carefully structured to produce the desired remainder interest; otherwise the assets may be totally depleted during the annuity term.

The term of a charitable annuity trust can be either for the life of an individual (or individuals) or for a term of years. Unlike the charitable remainder trust, lives and terms of years can be combined with a charitable lead annuity trust. However, the individual measuring life for an annuity trust must be alive at creation of the trust and must be the donor, the donor's spouse, or a person related to the non-charitable beneficiary.

Charitable Lead Unitrust (CLUT)

A charitable lead unitrust pays a set annual amount (expressed as a percentage) of the value of trust assets determined each year. Thus, the charity's payment will vary from year to year with the performance of trust assets. If the charitable lead unitrust's investments do not produce sufficient current income to make the payment, then principal of the trust must be paid out. There are no minimum or maximum payout percentages required.

The term of a charitable lead unitrust can be either for the life of an individual (or individuals) or for a term of years. It is possible to use lives and terms of years with a charitable lead unitrust. The individual measuring life for a unitrust must be alive at the creation of the trust and must be the donor, the donor's spouse, or a person related to the non-charitable beneficiary.

Generation-Skipping Transfer (GST) Tax

Careful planning is required if significant amounts of property are transferred to persons at least two generations younger than the grantor. Transfers that "skip" a generation can be subject to the generation-skipping transfer tax (GST tax). The tax can apply to all transfers, whether outright or in trust. Planning is key because the tax rate for generation-skipping transfers is equal to the highest estate and gift tax rate.

Each person has a lifetime exemption amount that can be transferred free of GST tax. Specific rules for calculating GST tax apply to charitable lead trusts. In general, these rules discourage the use of a charitable lead annuity trust as an appropriate vehicle to transfer wealth to grandchildren or future generations. However, a charitable lead *unitrust* can be a very powerful way to transfer wealth to grandchildren or future generations. Thus, a charitable lead unitrust is often created and funded with a donor's generation-skipping tax exemption amount in mind.

Example

Joe and Jane place appreciated securities with a value of $100,000 into a non-grantor charitable lead unitrust, which is to pay income to fund a scholarship at a private school. The payout is set at 10% of the annual value of the trust's assets for a term of 10 years. At the end of the 10 years, the remaining assets will pass to Joe's and Jane's grandchildren.

A taxable gift to the grandchildren results at the time the trust is established, but the gift tax is significantly reduced by the value of the income interest given to the school. Instead of a $100,000 gift, the income interest reduces the gift to $35,615 (calculated by using IRS tables in the month of contribution at the 8% assumed rate). In addition, upon the death of Joe and Jane, there is no additional estate tax and any appreciation in the securities after they were

(continues)

placed in trust is not subject to gift or estate taxation. No income tax charitable deduction is available for the contribution because Joe and Jane are not taxed on the trust's annual income; in other words, it is a non-grantor trust.

Observation

The transfer of the remainder interest to Joe's and Jane's grandchildren will be subject to the generation-skipping transfer tax. Thus, Joe and Jane must use some of their GST exemption when they create the trust.

Table 12.1 *Interest Rates: Impact on Gift Vehicles*

Gift Vehicle	Interest Rates Decline	Interest Rates Increase

Charitable remainder trust
  Annuity
  Unitrust
	
	Deduction decreases
	No impact
		
		Deduction increases
		No impact

Charitable lead trust
  Annuity
  Unitrust
	
	Deduction increases
	No impact
		
		Deduction decreases
		No impact

Charitable gift annuity	Deduction decreases	Deduction increases
Remainder interest in personal residence	Deduction increases	Deduction decreases
Pooled income fund	Deduction fluctuates	Deduction fluctuates

Chapter 13

Charitable Bequests

Just as charitable deductions during an individual's lifetime can produce sizable income tax savings, donations made at death can greatly reduce estate taxes. Other factors should also be considered, however, such as the intangible benefit of "supporting a charitable cause" through a lifetime gift versus establishing a legacy that will continue long after death.

Outright Bequests

The most common form of charitable bequest is a direct contribution or outright bequest directed in an individual's will or revocable trust. Charitable bequests are an effective estate tax–saving device because all transfers are fully deductible based on the fair market value of the property given to the charity. The restrictive rules that apply to transfers during life (i.e., percentage limitations and reduction rules) do not apply to transfers of assets at death. In addition, because the restrictive charitable deduction rules that apply to gifts to foreign charities do not apply to bequests to foreign charities, large amounts of assets can be bequeathed to foreign charities at death.

It is important to consider the impact of federal and state estate and inheritance taxes on the available deduction. The deductible amount is based on the bequest, but state law may require the amount to be reduced by taxes attributed to the bequest. Thus, decedents should state clearly in their wills whether a charitable transfer is liable for a share of death taxes.

Observation

Obviously, there are no current income tax deductions for charitable bequests.

Funding Charitable Bequests with Retirement Assets

Retirement assets produce ordinary income when received either before or after death and are known as assets that have "income in respect of a decedent," or IRD. Individual retirement accounts (IRAs), deferred compensation plan assets, and other pension plan assets are treated as IRD upon the death of the individual covered by the plan.

IRD items are subject to estate tax and the proceeds are subject to income tax when received by the beneficiaries. The combination of estate tax and income tax (including state income taxes) cause IRD type assets to be diminished by 70% or more. IRD items are inefficient assets to transfer to the next generation.

An alternative way to treat retirement assets is to use retirement plan benefits to fund charitable contributions. Estate tax is avoided because the amounts qualify for an estate tax charitable deduction. Income tax is avoided because the assets pass to an organization that is exempt from income tax.

	IRA at Death to Child	**IRA at Death to Charity**
Amount	$1,750,000	$1,750,000
Estate tax at 50%	875,000	0
Income tax*	306,250	0
Net to beneficiary	$568,750	$1,750,000

*Income tax: 35% × ($1,750,000 – 875,000) = $306,250. Because this is an IRD item for estate tax purposes, a deduction for estate taxes is available. Income tax on an IRD item is based on the gross amount less the estate tax attributable to that item.

Observation

Retirement assets are an excellent choice to leave to a charitable organization because these assets do not qualify for a step-up in basis either before or after the scheduled repeal of the estate tax. Additionally, because retirement assets generally don't qualify for capital gain rates, income tax consequences can be minimized by leaving these assets to charity.

Qualified Terminable Interest Property Trusts

In addition to outright bequests, individuals have the option of deferring a charitable bequest through the use of a qualified terminable interest property trust, commonly referred to as a QTIP trust. The QTIP trust allows an individual to make a substantial charitable contribution while providing a current income stream to a surviving spouse. The trust is usually set up in the individual's will or revocable trust. Upon the individual's death, the designated property is transferred to the trust, with the income paid to the surviving spouse on an annual or more frequent basis. Principal can also be made available to the surviving spouse as needed for health, education, support, or maintenance. Upon the death of the surviving spouse, the property passes to the charitable organization named.

This arrangement allows the property to pass totally free of estate taxes. There will be no estate tax upon the death of the first spouse because the transfer of property into trust for the benefit of the surviving spouse qualifies for the marital deduction. The marital deduction provides for an unlimited tax-free transfer of assets to the surviving spouse. Upon the death of the surviving spouse, the remaining trust property is included in the surviving spouse's estate, but the estate will receive an offsetting charitable deduction for estate tax purposes.

Figure 13.1 illustrates this "zero estate tax plan." Frank has $3 million. His goals are to provide for his spouse and child after his death and, ultimately, to make a sizable charitable gift.

Result: *No estate taxes in either estate.* The credit shelter trust results in no estate tax because it is designed to fully utilize the estate tax exemption amount. The credit shelter trust is not subject to estate tax upon the death of the surviving spouse—even if the surviving spouse is an income beneficiary.

The QTIP trust provides a marital deduction for Frank's estate resulting in no tax. Although the QTIP trust property is included in the surviving spouse's estate, it is offset for estate tax purposes by the charitable deduction created by the remainder passing to the charity. In addition, the trustee of the QTIP trust can make distributions of the trust principal to the surviving spouse for comfort and welfare in addition to required distributions of income.

Note that the estate tax exemption amount is adjusted from time to time. It is scheduled to increase from $1,000,000 in 2002 to $3,500,000 by 2009 at this writing.

Figure 13.1 *Zero Estate Tax Plan: QTIP Trust, Credit Shelter Trust, Charitable Remainder*

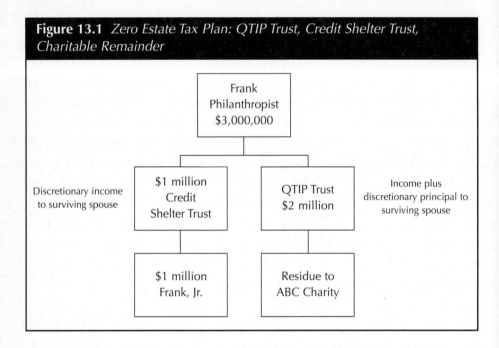

Chapter 14

Funding Contributions with Real Property

Alternative ways of donating real estate are discussed below. Examples high-light the tax ramifications of these alternatives, particularly as they apply to real estate that has appreciated in value. Note that there are significant differences between income-producing real estate and undeveloped real estate. Also, such gifts may be subject to extensive environmental studies before the charity is willing to accept them.

Outright Gift of Real Estate

As noted in other sections of this book, prospective donors should consider giving appreciated property, including real estate, rather than selling the property and donating the proceeds. Developed or undeveloped real estate is appropriate.

Gift of Partial Interest in Real Estate

Gifts of partial interests in real property enable individuals to make sizable donations without parting with cash. The partial interest must be expressed as a percentage of the total.

Either developed or undeveloped real estate is appropriate.

Example

Fred wishes to endow a faculty chair at his alma mater. The minimum donation for such an endowment is $200,000. He owns a tract of undeveloped land (zoned commercial) that is valued at $500,000. He donates a 40% interest in the property to the college. Fred receives a current $200,000 deduction. If Fred and his alma mater jointly sell the property at a later date, Fred will be required to pay tax on the gain attributable to his 60% interest in the property. The college will receive 40% of the sale price (enough to provide the $200,000 required to endow the scholarship).

Gift of Remainder Interest in Personal Residence or Farm

The transfer of the remainder interest in a personal residence (a vacation home would qualify) or farm to a charity can produce exceptional results for the donor. The donor not only retains full use of the property for the rest of his or her life (or a set period of years), but also receives a current income tax and a future estate tax charitable deduction.

Gift of Qualified Conservation Easement

The gift of a qualified conservation easement works well with a vacation property or other real property that has some unique conservation feature. For instance, property located near the boundaries of a national park or property that contains marshes or wetlands may be suited for such a transfer. The conservation easement would limit future options with respect to the property, but it is a unique way to make a gift of an interest in the property that is deductible for income and transfer tax purposes while retaining personal use of the property.

Bargain Sale

For many individuals, the bargain sale of real estate provides an excellent vehicle for charitable giving. The donor receives cash that can be used for reinvestment, avoids paying sales expenses, pays less capital gain tax than if the property was sold outright, and receives the benefit of a substantial charitable contribution. See "Bargain Sales" in Chapter 9.

Charitable Gift Annuity

A charitable gift annuity is an effective way to use real estate. Because the annuity payment is based on a flat rate upon contribution, the donor's return will not be affected by a future reduction in the property value. The charity will be able to pay the annuity from its overall income sources until the real property is sold.

Charitable Remainder Trust

Transfers of undeveloped real estate into a charitable remainder trust can be troubling unless the undeveloped real property is sold soon after the contribution. The problem with non–income-producing real estate is the real estate taxes that are due periodically. The charity should not pay the real estate tax, nor should the donor.

An income-only unitrust provides a good alternative to selling undeveloped real property immediately. The income-only unitrust is ideally suited for gifts of low income-producing real estate because the makeup feature will allow the donor to recoup the difference between the income produced and the fair market value of the trust assets (when the property is sold) at a later date. Further, because the unitrust can accept additional contributions, the donor's payment of real estate taxes can be viewed as added contributions.

Income-producing real property can also be contributed to a charitable remainder trust. There may be significant tax concerns if the property has debt associated with it. See discussion in Chapter 11.

Pooled Income Fund

Although real property can be contributed to many pooled income funds (donors need to check with the applicable charity), long-term charitable results may be impaired. High-value real estate that produces little income may adversely affect pooled income fund results if the real estate is not sold soon.

Charitable Lead Trust

Funding a charitable lead trust with income-producing real property works particularly well with property that is likely to appreciate in value. The value of the gift to the non-charitable remainder beneficiaries for gift and estate tax purposes is based on the value of the property when the trust is established, less the income interest paid to the charity over the term of the trust. The lead interest should be linked to the income produced by the property each year to prevent having portions of the underlying property transferred to the charity.

Appendix A

Charitable Giving Alternatives

Charitable Remainder Trust

Split-interest irrevocable trust that has charitable and non-charitable beneficiaries. An individual donor transfers property to the trust, which guarantees to pay the individual or a designated non-charitable beneficiary a fixed percentage of the fair market value of the trust's assets for life or a term of years. At the termination of the non-charitable beneficiary's interest, remaining trust assets are passed to a qualifying charity.

Purposes

- The donor desires to make charitable contributions.
- The donor wants to reduce current income taxes.
- The donor seeks to reduce estate taxes.
- The donor desires to retain income generated by the contributed property.

Advantages

- Provides the charity with assets in the future.
- Grants the donor a current charitable deduction for the value of the property transferred to the charity in the future.

- Reduces donor's taxable estate.
- Provides the donor or designated beneficiary with a current income stream.

Disadvantages

- Donated assets pass to charity instead of heirs.
- The charity must wait to receive donated assets.

Charitable Lead Trust

Split-interest irrevocable trust that has charitable and non-charitable beneficiaries. An individual donor transfers property to the trust, which guarantees to pay the charity a fixed percentage of the fair market value of the trust's assets for a term of years. At the termination of the charitable beneficiary's interest, remaining trust assets are passed to a designated non-charitable beneficiary (donor or family member).

Purposes

- The donor desires to make charitable contributions.
- The donor wants to reduce current income taxes as it is earned by the trust.
- The donor seeks to reduce estate or gift taxes.
- The donor desires to retain the property contributed.

Advantages

- Provides the charity with current income.
- Grants the donor a current charitable deduction for all payments to be made to the charity if donor is taxed on income as it is earned by the trust.
- Allows the donor or designated beneficiaries to retain donated assets.
- Provides the opportunity to reduce the donor's estate.

Disadvantages

- The donor may be taxed on the trust's income.
- The donor loses control of the assets during the term of the charity's interest.

Charitable Gift Annuity

A contractual arrangement between an individual and a charity. It provides the donor or other designated individual(s) with an annuity for life in exchange for the transfer of property to charity.

Purposes

- The donor desires to make charitable contributions.
- The donor wants to reduce income taxes.
- The donor seeks to reduce estate taxes.
- The donor desires income from the contributed property.

Advantages

- Grants the donor a current charitable deduction.
- Reduces the donor's taxable estate.
- Provides the donor with a current income stream.
- Provides the charity with current assets.
- Requires less tax compliance than charitable remainder or lead trusts.

Disadvantages

- Donated assets pass to charity instead of heirs.
- Transaction is treated in part as a charitable contribution and in part as the purchase of an annuity.

Remainder Interest in a Personal Residence or Farm

A gift of a remainder interest in a personal residence or farm to a qualified charitable organization. The individual donor agrees to transfer his or her personal residence or farm to the charity after a term of years or life. The donor lives in or uses the house or farm during this term of years or life. At the end of the donor's interest, the property is passed to the charity.

Purposes

- The donor desires to make charitable contributions.
- The donor wants to reduce income taxes.
- The donor seeks to reduce estate taxes.
- The donor wants to live in or use the property.
- The charity requires property.

Advantages

- Provides the charity with future real estate for growth and expansion.
- Grants the donor a current charitable deduction.
- Reduces the donor's taxable estate.
- Allows the donor to live in or use the house or farm for a term of years or life.

Disadvantages

- Donated property passes to charity instead of heirs.
- Charity must wait to receive the real estate.
- Gain on sale of primary residence exclusion may be lost.

Appendix B

Form 8282—Donee Information Return (and Instructions)

Form **8282**	**Donee Information Return**	OMB No. 1545-0908
(Rev. September 1998) Department of the Treasury Internal Revenue Service	(Sale, Exchange, or Other Disposition of Donated Property) ▶ See instructions on back.	Give a Copy to Donor

Please Print or Type	Name of charitable organization (donee)	Employer identification number
	Address (number, street, and room or suite no.)	
	City or town, state, and ZIP code	

Part I — Information on ORIGINAL DONOR and DONEE Receiving the Property

1a Name(s) of the original donor of the property	1b Identifying number

Note: Complete lines 2a–2d only if you gave this property to another charitable organization (successor donee).

2a Name of charitable organization	2b Employer identification number
2c Address (number, street, and room or suite no.)	
2d City or town, state, and ZIP code	

Note: If you are the original donee, skip Part II and go to Part III now.

Part II — Information on PREVIOUS DONEES—Complete this part only if you were not the first donee to receive the property.

If you were the second donee, leave lines 4a–4d blank. If you were a third or later donee, complete lines 3a–4d. On lines 4a–4d, give information on the preceding donee (the one who gave you the property).

3a Name of original donee	3b Employer identification number
3c Address (number, street, and room or suite no.)	
3d City or town, state, and ZIP code	
4a Name of preceding donee	4b Employer identification number
4c Address (number, street, and room or suite no.)	
4d City or town, state, and ZIP code	

Part III — Information on DONATED PROPERTY—If you are the original donee, leave column (c) blank.

(a) Description of donated property sold, exchanged, or otherwise disposed of (if you need more space, attach a separate statement)	(b) Date you received the item(s)	(c) Date the first donee received the item(s)	(d) Date item(s) sold, exchanged, or otherwise disposed of	(e) Amount received upon disposition

For Paperwork Reduction Act Notice, see back of form.	Cat. No. 62307Y	Form **8282** (Rev. 9-98)

General Instructions

Section references are to the Internal Revenue Code.

Purpose of Form

Donee organizations use Form 8282 to report information to the IRS about dispositions of certain charitable deduction property made within 2 years after the donor contributed the property.

Definitions

Note: *For Form 8282 and these instructions, the term "donee" includes all donees, unless specific reference is made to "original" or "successor" donees.*

Original donee. The first donee to or for which the donor gave the property. The original donee is required to sign an Appraisal Summary presented by the donor for charitable deduction property.

Successor donee. Any donee of property other than the original donee.

Appraisal summary. Section B of Form **8283,** Noncash Charitable Contributions.

Charitable deduction property. Property (other than money or certain publicly traded securities) for which the original donee signed, as an appraised value for signature, the Appraisal Summary (Form 8283, Section B).

Generally, only items or groups of similar items for which the donor claimed a deduction of more than $5,000 are included on the Appraisal Summary. There is an exception if a donor gives similar items to more than one donee organization and the total deducted for these similar items exceeds $5,000. For example, if a donor deducts $2,000 for books given to a donee organization and $4,000 for books to another donee organization, the donor must present a separate Appraisal Summary to each organization. For more information, see the Instructions for Form 8283.

Who Must File

Original and successor donee organizations must file Form 8282 if they sell, exchange, consume, or otherwise dispose of (with or without consideration) charitable deduction property within 2 years after the date the original donee received the property. See **Charitable deduction property** earlier.

Exceptions. There are two situations where Form 8282 does not have to be filed.

1. Items valued at $500 or less. You do not have to file Form 8282 if, at the time the original donee signed the Appraisal Summary, the donor had signed a statement on Form 8283 that the appraised value of the specific item was not more than $500. If Form 8283 contains more than one similar item, this exception applies only to those items that are clearly identified as having a value of $500 or less. However, for purposes of the donor's

determination of whether the appraised value of the item exceeds $500, all shares of nonpublicly traded stock, or items that form a set, are considered one item. For example, a collection of books written by the same author, components of a stereo system, or six place settings of a pattern of silverware are considered one item.

2. Items consumed or distributed for charitable purpose. You do not have to file Form 8282 if an item is consumed or distributed, without consideration, in fulfilling your purpose or function as a tax-exempt organization. For example, no reporting is required for medical supplies consumed or distributed by a tax-exempt relief organization in aiding disaster victims.

When To File

If you dispose of charitable deduction property within 2 years of the date the original donee received it and you do not meet exception **1** or **2** above, you must file Form 8282 within 125 days after the date of disposition.

Exception. If you did not file because you had no reason to believe the substantiation requirements applied to the donor, but you later become aware that they did apply, file Form 8282 within 60 days after the date you become aware you are liable. For example, this exception would apply where an Appraisal Summary is furnished to a successor donee after the date that donee disposes of the charitable deduction property.

Missing Information

If Form 8282 is filed by the due date, you must enter your organization's name, address, and EIN and complete at least Part III, column (a). You do not have to complete the remaining items if the information is not available. For example, you may not have the information necessary to complete all entries if the donor's Appraisal Summary is not available to you.

Where To File

Send Form 8282 to the Internal Revenue Service, Ogden, UT 84201-0027.

Penalty

You may be subject to a penalty if you fail to file this form by the due date, fail to include all of the information required to be shown on this form, or fail to include correct information on this form (see **Missing Information** above). The penalty is generally $50. For more details, see section 6721.

Other Requirements

Information you must give a successor donee. If the property is transferred to another charitable organization within the 2-year period discussed earlier, you must give your successor donee all of the following information.

1. The name, address, and EIN of your organization.

2. A copy of the Appraisal Summary (the Form 8283 that you received from the donor or a preceding donee).

3. A copy of this Form 8282, within 15 days after you file it.

You must furnish items **1** and **2** above within 15 days after the latest of the date:

● You transferred the property,

● The original donee signed the Appraisal Summary, or

● You received a copy of the Appraisal Summary from the preceding donee if you are also a successor donee.

Information the successor donee must give you. The successor donee organization to whom you transferred this property is required to give you their organization's name, address, and EIN within 15 days after the later of:

● The date you transferred the property, or

● The date they received a copy of the Appraisal Summary.

Information you must give the donor. You must give a copy of your Form 8282 to the original donor of the property.

Recordkeeping. You must keep a copy of the Appraisal Summary in your records.

Paperwork Reduction Act Notice. We ask for the information on this form to carry out the Internal Revenue laws of the United States. You are required to give us the information. We need it to ensure that you are complying with these laws and to allow us to figure and collect the right amount of tax.

You are not required to provide the information requested on a form that is subject to the Paperwork Reduction Act unless the form displays a valid OMB control number. Books or records relating to a form or its instructions must be retained as long as their contents may become material in the administration of any Internal Revenue law. Generally, tax returns and return information are confidential, as required by section 6103.

The time needed to complete this form will vary depending on individual circumstances. The estimated average time is:

Recordkeeping . . . . 3 hr., 7 min.

Learning about the law or the form . . . . 35 min.

Preparing and sending the form to the IRS . . . . . 41 min.

If you have comments concerning the accuracy of these time estimates or suggestions for making this form simpler, we would be happy to hear from you. You can write to the Tax Forms Committee, Western Area Distribution Center, Rancho Cordova, CA 95743-0001. **DO NOT** send the form to this address. Instead, see **Where To File** on this page.

Appendix C

Form 8283—Noncash Charitable Contributions (and Instructions)

Form **8283** (Rev. October 1998) Department of the Treasury Internal Revenue Service	**Noncash Charitable Contributions** ▶ Attach to your tax return if you claimed a total deduction of over $500 for all contributed property. ▶ See separate instructions.	OMB No. 1545-0908 Attachment Sequence No. **55**
Name(s) shown on your income tax return		Identifying number

Note: *Figure the amount of your contribution deduction before completing this form. See your tax return instructions.*

Section A—List in this section **only** items (or groups of similar items) for which you claimed a deduction of $5,000 or less. Also, list certain publicly traded securities even if the deduction is over $5,000 (see instructions).

Part I **Information on Donated Property**—If you need more space, attach a statement.

1	(a) Name and address of the donee organization	(b) Description of donated property
A		
B		
C		
D		
E		

Note: *If the amount you claimed as a deduction for an item is $500 or less, you do not have to complete columns (d), (e), and (f).*

	(c) Date of the contribution	(d) Date acquired by donor (mo., yr.)	(e) How acquired by donor	(f) Donor's cost or adjusted basis	(g) Fair market value	(h) Method used to determine the fair market value
A						
B						
C						
D						
E						

Part II **Other Information**—Complete line 2 if you gave less than an entire interest in property listed in Part I. Complete line 3 if conditions were attached to a contribution listed in Part I.

2 If, during the year, you contributed less than the entire interest in the property, complete lines a–e.

a Enter the letter from Part I that identifies the property ▶ _____. If Part II applies to more than one property, attach a separate statement.

b Total amount claimed as a deduction for the property listed in Part I: **(1)** For this tax year ▶ _____ .
                                  (2) For any prior tax years ▶ _____ .

c Name and address of each organization to which any such contribution was made in a prior year (complete only if different from the donee organization above):

Name of charitable organization (donee)

Address (number, street, and room or suite no.)

City or town, state, and ZIP code

d For tangible property, enter the place where the property is located or kept ▶ _____

e Name of any person, other than the donee organization, having actual possession of the property ▶ _____

3 If conditions were attached to any contribution listed in Part I, answer questions a – c and attach the required statement (see instructions).

		Yes	No
a	Is there a restriction, either temporary or permanent, on the donee's right to use or dispose of the donated property?		
b	Did you give to anyone (other than the donee organization or another organization participating with the donee organization in cooperative fundraising) the right to the income from the donated property or to the possession of the property, including the right to vote donated securities, to acquire the property by purchase or otherwise, or to designate the person having such income, possession, or right to acquire?		
c	Is there a restriction limiting the donated property for a particular use?		

For Paperwork Reduction Act Notice, see page 4 of separate instructions.   Cat. No. 62299J   Form **8283** (Rev. 10-98)

Form 8283 (Rev. 10-98) | Page **2**

Name(s) shown on your income tax return | Identifying number

Section B—Appraisal Summary—List in this section only items (or groups of similar items) for which you claimed a deduction of more than $5,000 per item or group. **Exception.** Report contributions of certain publicly traded securities only in Section A.

If you donated art, you may have to attach the complete appraisal. See the **Note** in Part I below.

Part I Information on Donated Property—To be completed by the taxpayer and/or appraiser.

4 Check type of property:

☐ Art* (contribution of $20,000 or more) ☐ Real Estate ☐ Gems/Jewelry ☐ Stamp Collections
☐ Art* (contribution of less than $20,000) ☐ Coin Collections ☐ Books ☐ Other

*Art includes paintings, sculptures, watercolors, prints, drawings, ceramics, antique furniture, decorative arts, textiles, carpets, silver, rare manuscripts, historical memorabilia, and other similar objects.

Note: If your total art contribution deduction was $20,000 or more, you must attach a complete copy of the signed appraisal. See instructions.

5	(a) Description of donated property (if you need more space, attach a separate statement)	(b) If tangible property was donated, give a brief summary of the overall physical condition at the time of the gift	(c) Appraised fair market value
A			
B			
C			
D			

	(d) Date acquired by donor (mo., yr.)	(e) How acquired by donor	(f) Donor's cost or adjusted basis	(g) For bargain sales, enter amount received	(h) Amount claimed as a deduction	(i) Average trading price of securities
A						
B						
C						
D						

Part II Taxpayer (Donor) Statement—List each item included in Part I above that the appraisal identifies as having a value of $500 or less. See instructions.

I declare that the following item(s) included in Part I above has to the best of my knowledge and belief an appraised value of not more than $500 (per item). Enter identifying letter from Part I and describe the specific item. See instructions. ▶ _____

Signature of taxpayer (donor) ▶ Date ▶

Part III Declaration of Appraiser

I declare that I am not the donor, the donee, a party to the transaction in which the donor acquired the property, employed by, or related to any of the foregoing persons, or married to any person who is related to any of the foregoing persons. And, if regularly used by the donor, donee, or party to the transaction, I performed the majority of my appraisals during my tax year for other persons.

Also, I declare that I hold myself out to the public as an appraiser or perform appraisals on a regular basis; and that because of my qualifications as described in the appraisal, I am qualified to make appraisals of the type of property being valued. I certify that the appraisal fees were not based on a percentage of the appraised property value. Furthermore, I understand that a false or fraudulent overstatement of the property value as described in the qualified appraisal or this appraisal summary may subject me to the penalty under section 6701(a) (aiding and abetting the understatement of tax liability). I affirm that I have not been barred from presenting evidence or testimony by the Director of Practice.

Sign Here Signature ▶ Title ▶ Date of appraisal ▶

Business address (including room or suite no.) | Identifying number

City or town, state, and ZIP code

Part IV Donee Acknowledgment—To be completed by the charitable organization.

This charitable organization acknowledges that it is a qualified organization under section 170(c) and that it received the donated property as described in Section B, Part I, above on ▶ _____ (Date)

Furthermore, this organization affirms that in the event it sells, exchanges, or otherwise disposes of the property described in Section B, Part I (or any portion thereof) within 2 years after the date of receipt, it will file **Form 8282,** Donee Information Return, with the IRS and give the donor a copy of that form. This acknowledgment does not represent agreement with the claimed fair market value.

Does the organization intend to use the property for an unrelated use? . . . . ▶ ☐ Yes ☐ No

Name of charitable organization (donee)	Employer identification number	
Address (number, street, and room or suite no.)	City or town, state, and ZIP code	
Authorized signature	Title	Date

Instructions for Form 8283

(Revised October 1998)

Noncash Charitable Contributions

Section references are to the Internal Revenue Code unless otherwise noted.

Department of the Treasury
Internal Revenue Service

General Instructions

Purpose of Form

Use Form 8283 to report information about noncash charitable contributions.

Do not use Form 8283 to report out-of-pocket expenses for volunteer work or amounts you gave by check or credit card. Treat these items as cash contributions. Also, **do not** use Form 8283 to figure your charitable contribution deduction. For details on how to figure the amount of the deduction, see your tax return instructions.

Additional Information

You may want to see **Pub. 526,** Charitable Contributions (for individuals), and **Pub. 561,** Determining the Value of Donated Property. If you contributed depreciable property, see **Pub. 544,** Sales and Other Dispositions of Assets.

Who Must File

You must file Form 8283 if the amount of your deduction for all noncash gifts is more than $500. For this purpose, "amount of your deduction" means your deduction **before** applying any income limits that could result in a carryover. The carryover rules are explained in Pub. 526. Make any required reductions to fair market value (FMV) before you determine if you must file Form 8283. See **Fair Market Value (FMV)** on page 2.

Form 8283 is filed by individuals, partnerships, and corporations.

Note: *C corporations, other than personal service corporations and closely held corporations, must file Form 8283 only if the amount claimed as a deduction is over $5,000.*

Partnerships and S corporations. A partnership or S corporation that claims a deduction for noncash gifts over $500 must file Form 8283 with Form 1065, 1065-B, or 1120S. If the total deduction of any item or group of similar items exceeds $5,000, the partnership or S corporation must complete Section B of Form 8283 even if the amount allocated to each partner or shareholder does not exceed $5,000.

The partnership or S corporation must give a completed copy of Form 8283 to each partner or shareholder receiving an allocation of the contribution deduction shown in Section B of the partnership's or S corporation's Form 8283.

Partners and shareholders. The partnership or S corporation will provide information about your share of the contribution on your Schedule K-1 (Form 1065 or 1120S).

In some cases, the partnership or S corporation must give you a copy of its Form 8283. If you received a copy of Form 8283 from the partnership or S corporation, attach a copy to your tax return. Deduct the amount shown on your Schedule K-1, not the amount shown on the Form 8283.

If the partnership or S corporation is not required to give you a copy of its Form 8283, combine the amount of noncash contributions shown on your Schedule K-1 with your other noncash contributions to see if you must file Form 8283. If you need to file Form 8283, you do not have to complete all the information requested in Section A for your share of the partnership's or S corporation's contributions. Complete only column (g) of line 1 with your share of the contribution and enter "From Schedule K-1 (Form 1065 or 1120S)" across columns (c)–(f).

When To File

File Form 8283 with your tax return for the year you contribute the property and first claim a deduction.

Which Sections To Complete

If you must file Form 8283, you may need to complete Section A, Section B, or both, depending on the type of property donated and the amount claimed as a deduction.

Section A. Include in Section A only items (or groups of similar items as defined on this page) for which you claimed a deduction of $5,000 or less per item (or group of similar items). Also, include the following publicly traded securities even if the deduction is more than $5,000.

● Securities listed on an exchange in which quotations are published daily,

● Securities regularly traded in national or regional over-the-counter markets for which published quotations are available, or

● Securities that are shares of a mutual fund for which quotations are published on a daily basis in a newspaper of general circulation throughout the United States.

Section B. Include in Section B only items (or groups of similar items) for which you claimed a deduction of more than $5,000 (omit publicly traded securities reportable in Section A). With certain exceptions, items reported in Section B will require information based on a written appraisal by a qualified appraiser.

Similar Items of Property

Similar items of property are items of the same generic category or type, such as stamp collections, coin collections, lithographs, paintings, books, nonpublicly traded stock, land, or buildings.

Example. You claimed a deduction of $400 for clothing, $7,000 for publicly traded securities (quotations published daily), and $6,000 for a collection of 15 books ($400 each). Report the clothing and securities in Section A and the books (a group of similar items) in Section B.

Special Rule for Certain C Corporations

A special rule applies for deductions taken by certain C corporations under section 170(e)(3) or (4) for contributions of inventory or scientific equipment.

Cat. No. 62730R

To determine if you must file Form 8283 or which section to complete, use the difference between the amount you claimed as a deduction and the amount you would have claimed as cost of goods sold (COGS) had you sold the property instead. This rule is **only** for purposes of Form 8283. It does not change the amount or method of figuring your contribution deduction.

If you do not have to file Form 8283 because of this rule, you must attach a statement to your tax return (similar to the one in the example below). Also, attach a statement if you must complete Section A, instead of Section B, because of this rule.

Example. You donated clothing from your inventory for the care of the needy. The clothing cost you $5,000 and your claimed charitable deduction is $8,000. Complete Section A instead of Section B because the difference between the amount you claimed as a charitable deduction and the amount that would have been your COGS deduction is $3,000 ($8,000 − $5,000). Attach a statement to Form 8283 similar to the following:

Form 8283—Inventory

Contribution deduction	$8,000
COGS (if sold, not donated)	− 5,000
For Form 8283 filing purposes	=$3,000

Fair Market Value (FMV)

Although the **amount** of your deduction determines if you have to file Form 8283, you also need to have information about the **value** of your contribution to complete the form.

FMV is the price a willing, knowledgeable buyer would pay a willing, knowledgeable seller when neither has to buy or sell.

You may not always be able to deduct the FMV of your contribution. Depending on the type of property donated, you may have to reduce the FMV to get to the deductible amount, as explained next.

Reductions to FMV. The amount of the reduction (if any) depends on whether the property is ordinary income property or capital gain property. Attach a statement to your tax return showing how you figured the reduction.

Ordinary income property is property that would result in ordinary income or short-term capital gain if it were sold at its FMV on the date it was contributed. Examples of ordinary income property are inventory, works of art created by the donor, and capital assets held for 1 year or less. The deduction for a gift of ordinary income property is limited to the FMV minus the amount that would be ordinary income or short-term capital gain if the property were sold.

Capital gain property is property that would result in long-term capital gain if it were sold at its FMV on the date it was contributed. It includes certain real property and depreciable property used in your trade or business, and generally may deduct gifts of capital gain property at their FMV. However, you must reduce the FMV by the amount of any appreciation if any of the following apply.

The capital gain property is contributed to certain private nonoperating foundations. This rule does not apply to qualified appreciated stock.

You choose the 50% limit instead of the special 30% limit.

The contributed property is tangible personal property that is put to an **unrelated use** (as defined in Pub. 526) by the charity.

Qualified conservation contribution. If your donation qualifies as a "qualified conservation contribution" under section 170(h), attach a statement showing the FMV of the underlying property before and after the gift and the conservation purpose furthered by the gift. See Pub. 561 for more details.

Specific Instructions

Identifying number. Individuals must enter their social security number or individual taxpayer identification number. All other filers should enter their employer identification number.

Section A

Part I, Information on Donated Property

Line 1

Column (b). Describe the property in sufficient detail. The greater the value, the more detail you need. For example, a car should be described in more detail than pots and pans.

For securities, include the following:

Name of the issuer,

Kind of security,

Whether a share of a mutual fund, and

Whether regularly traded on a stock exchange or in an over-the-counter market.

Note: *If the amount you claimed as a deduction for the item is $500 or less, you do not have to complete columns (d), (e), and (f).*

Column (d). Enter the approximate date you acquired the property. If it was created, produced, or manufactured by or for you, enter the date it was substantially completed.

Column (e). State how you acquired the property (i.e., by purchase, gift, inheritance, or exchange).

Column (f). **Do not** complete this column for publicly traded securities or property held 12 months or more. Keep records on cost or other basis.

Note: *If you have reasonable cause for not providing the information in columns (d) and (f), attach an explanation.*

Column (g). Enter the FMV of the property on the date you donated it. If you were required to reduce the FMV of your deduction or you gave a qualified conservation contribution, you must attach a statement. See **Fair Market Value (FMV)** on this page for the type of statement to attach.

Column (h). Enter the method(s) you used to determine the FMV. The FMV of used household goods and clothing is usually much lower than when new. A good measure of value might be the price that buyers of these used items actually pay in consignment or thrift shops.

Examples of entries to make include "Appraisal," "Thrift shop value" (for clothing or household goods), "Catalog" (for stamp or coin collections), or "Comparable sales" (for real estate and other kinds of assets). See Pub. 561.

Part II, Other Information

If Part II applies to more than one property, attach a separate statement. Give the required information for each property separately. Identify which property listed in Part I the information relates to.

Lines 2a Through 2e

Complete lines 2a–2e only if you contributed less than the entire interest in the donated property during the tax year. On line 2b, enter the amount claimed as a deduction for this tax year and in any prior tax years for gifts of a partial interest in the same property.

Lines 3a Through 3c

Complete lines 3a–3c only if you attached restrictions to the right to the income, use, or disposition of the donated property. An example of a "restricted use" is furniture that you gave only to be used in the reading room of an organization's library. Attach a statement explaining **(1)** the terms of any agreement or understanding regarding the restriction, and **(2)** whether the property is designated for a particular use.

Section B

Part I, Information on Donated Property

You must have a written appraisal from a qualified appraiser that supports the information in Part I. However, see the **Exceptions** below.

Use Part I to summarize your appraisal(s). Generally, you do not need to attach the appraisals but you should keep them for your records. But see **Art valued at $20,000 or more** below.

Exceptions. You do not need a written appraisal if the property is:

• Nonpublicly traded stock of $10,000 or less,

• Certain securities considered to have market quotations readily available (see Regulations section 1.170A-13(c)(7)(xi)(B)),

• A donation by a C corporation (other than a closely held corporation or personal service corporation), or

• Inventory and other property donated by a closely held corporation or a personal service corporation that are "qualified contributions" for the care of the ill, the needy, or infants, within the meaning of section 170(e)(3)(A).

Although a written appraisal is not required for the types of property listed above, you must provide certain information in Part I of Section B (see Regulations section 1.170A-13(c)(4)(iv)) and have the donee organization complete Part IV.

Art valued at $20,000 or more. If your total deduction for art is $20,000 or more, you must attach a complete copy of the signed appraisal. For individual objects valued at $20,000 or more, a photograph must be provided upon request. The photograph must be of sufficient quality and size (preferably an 8 x 10 inch color photograph or a color transparency no smaller than 4 x 5 inches) to fully show the object.

Appraisal Requirements

The appraisal must be made not earlier than 60 days before the date you contribute the property. You must receive the appraisal before the due date (including extensions) of the return on which you first claim a deduction for the property. For a deduction first claimed on an amended return, the appraisal must be received before the date the amended return was filed.

A separate qualified appraisal and a separate Form 8283 are required for each item of property except for an item that is part of a group of similar items. Only one appraisal is required for a group of similar items contributed in the same tax year, if it includes all the required information for each item. The appraiser may group similar items with a collective value appraised at $100 or less.

If you gave similar items to more than one donee for which you claimed a total deduction of more than $5,000, you must attach a separate form for each donee.

Example. You claimed a deduction of $2,000 for books given to College A, $2,500 for books given to College B, and $900 for books given to a public library. You must attach a separate Form 8283 for each donee.

See Regulations section 1.170A-13(c)(3)(i)–(ii) for the definition of a "qualified appraisal" and information to be included in the appraisal.

Line 5

Note: *You must complete at least column (a) of line 5 (and column (b) if applicable) before submitting Form 8283 to the donee. You may then complete the remaining columns.*

Column (a). Provide enough detail so a person unfamiliar with the property could identify it in the appraisal.

Column (c). Include the FMV from the appraisal. If you were not required to get an appraisal, include the FMV you determine to be correct.

Columns (d)–(f). If you have reasonable cause for not providing the information in columns (d), (e), or (f), attach an explanation so your deduction will not automatically be disallowed.

Column (g). A bargain sale is a transfer of property that is in part a sale or exchange and in part a contribution. Enter the amount received for bargain sales.

Column (h). Complete column (h) only if you were not required to get an appraisal, as explained earlier.

Column (i). Complete column (i) only if you donated securities for which market quotations are considered to be readily available because the issue satisfies the five requirements described in Regulations section 1.170A-13(c)(7)(xi)(B).

Part II, Taxpayer (Donor) Statement

Complete Part II for each item included in Part I that has an appraised value of $500 or less. Because you do not have to show the value of these items in Part I of the donee's copy of Form 8283, clearly identify them for the donee in Part II. Then, the donee does not have to file **Form 8282,** Donee Information Return, for items valued at $500 or less. See the **Note** on page 4 for more details about filing Form 8282.

The amount of information you give in Part II depends on the description of the donated property you enter in Part I. If you show a single item as "Property A" in Part I and that item is appraised at $500 or less, then the entry "Property A" in Part II is enough. However, if "Property A" consists of several items and the total appraised value is over $500, list in Part II any item(s) you gave that is valued at $500 or less.

All shares of nonpublicly traded stock or items in a set are considered one item. For example, a book collection by the same author, components of a stereo system, or six place settings of a pattern of silverware are one item for the $500 test.

Example. You donated books valued at $6,000. The appraisal states that one of the items, a collection of books by author "X," is worth $400. On the Form 8283 that you are required to give the donee, you decide not to show the appraised value of all of the books. But you also do not want the donee to have to file Form 8282 if the collection of books is sold. If your description of Property A on line 5 includes all the books, then specify in Part II the "collection of books by X included in Property A." But if your Property A description is "collection of books by X," the only required entry in Part II is "Property A."

In the above example, you may have chosen instead to give a completed copy of Form 8283 to the donee. The donee would then be aware of the value. If you include all the books as Property A on line 5, and enter $6,000 in column (c), you may still want to describe the specific collection in Part II so the donee can sell it without filing Form 8282.

Part III, Declaration of Appraiser

If you had to get an appraisal, the appraiser **must** complete Part III to be considered qualified. See Regulations section 1.170A-13(c)(5) for a definition of a qualified appraiser.

Persons who cannot be qualified appraisers are listed in the Declaration of Appraiser. Usually, a party to the transaction will not qualify to sign the declaration. But a person who sold, exchanged, or gave the property to you may sign the declaration if the property was donated within 2 months of the date you acquired it and the property's appraised value did not exceed its acquisition price.

An appraiser may not be considered qualified if you had knowledge of facts that would cause a reasonable person to expect the appraiser to falsely overstate the value of the property. An example of this is an agreement between you and the appraiser about the property value when you know that the appraised amount exceeds the actual FMV.

Usually, appraisal fees cannot be based on a percentage of the appraised value unless the fees were paid to certain not-for-profit associations. See Regulations section 1.170A-13(c)(6)(ii).

Part IV, Donee Acknowledgment

The donee organization that received the property described in Part I of Section B must complete Part IV. Before submitting page 2 of Form 8283 to the donee for acknowledgment, complete at least your name, identifying number, and description of the donated property (line 5, column (a)). If tangible property is donated, also describe its physical condition (line 5, column (b)) at the time of the gift. Complete Part II, if applicable, before submitting form to the donee. See the instructions for Part II.

The person acknowledging the gift must be an official authorized to sign the tax returns of the organization, or a person specifically designated to sign Form 8283. After completing Part IV, the organization must return Form 8283 to you, the donor. You must give a copy of Section B of this form to the donee organization. You may then complete any remaining information required in Part I. Also, Part III may be completed at this time by the qualified appraiser.

In some cases, it may be impossible to get the donee's signature on the Appraisal Summary. The deduction will not be disallowed for that reason if you attach a detailed explanation why it was impossible.

Note: *If the donee (or a successor donee) organization disposes of the property within 2 years after the date the original donee received it, the organization must file **Form 8282**, Donee Information Return, with the IRS and send a copy to the donor. An exception applies to items having a value of $500 or less if the donor identified the items and signed the statement in Part II (Section B) of Form 8283. See the instructions for Part II.*

Failure To File Form 8283, Section B

If you fail to attach Form 8283 to your return for donated property that is required to be reported in Section B, your deduction will be disallowed unless your failure was due to a good-faith omission. If the IRS asks you to submit the form, you have 90 days to send a completed Section B of Form 8283 before your deduction is disallowed.

Paperwork Reduction Act Notice. We ask for the information on this form to carry out the Internal Revenue laws of the United States. You are required to give us the information. We need it to ensure that you are complying with these laws and to allow us to figure and collect the right amount of tax.

You are not required to provide the information requested on a form that is subject to the Paperwork Reduction Act unless the form displays a valid OMB control number. Books or records relating to a form or its instructions must be retained as long as their contents may become material in the administration of any Internal Revenue law. Generally, tax returns and return information are confidential, as required by section 6103.

The time needed to complete and file this form will vary depending on individual circumstances. The estimated average time is: **Recordkeeping**, 20 min.; **Learning about the law or the form**, 29 min.; **Preparing the form**, 37 min.; **Copying, assembling, and sending the form to the IRS**, 35 min.

If you have comments concerning the accuracy of these time estimates or suggestions for making this form simpler, we would be happy to hear from you. See the instructions for the tax return with which this form is filed.

Appendix D

IRS Publication 3833—
Disaster Relief: Providing Assistance through Charitable Organizations

Disaster Relief: Providing Assistance through Charitable Organizations is for people interested in using a charitable organization to provide help to victims of disasters or other emergency hardship situations. These disasters may be caused by floods, fires, riots, storms, or similar large-scale events. Emergency hardship may be caused by illness, death, accident, violent crime, or other personal events. This publication includes:

- advice about helping to provide relief through an existing charitable organization
- information about establishing a new charitable organization
- guidance about how charitable organizations can help victims
- requirements for documentation
- a special statutory rule that applies only to disaster relief assistance for victims of the September 11, 2001, terrorist attacks on the United States
- guidance about employer-sponsored assistance programs
- information about gifts and charitable contribution rules
- reference publications and sources of assistance

By using this publication at an early stage to help plan your relief efforts, your program will be able to help victims in ways that are consistent with the federal tax rules that apply to charities.

Providing aid to relieve human suffering that may be caused by a natural or civil disaster or an emergency hardship is charity in its most basic form. Charitable organizations, including churches, are frequently able to administer relief programs more efficiently than individuals acting on their own. Charitable organizations can offer assistance over long periods of time. Even if the charity later dissolves, its remaining assets are permanently dedicated to accomplishing charitable purposes and cannot be divided among the organization's members, directors, or employees.

Of course, there are tax advantages when relief is provided by a charitable organization that qualifies for tax-exempt status. Being exempt from federal income tax reduces an organization's expenses, which may allow additional resources to be used to accomplish its mission. Plus, contributors to qualified charitable organizations may be eligible to claim tax deductions for their donations, and the value of these contributions is not subject to gift tax, regardless of the amount. In general, individuals who receive assistance in meeting personal needs from a charitable organization are not subject to federal income tax on the value of the assistance.

Helping through an Existing Charitable Organization

A tragic event can often prompt an outpouring of assistance. In the rush to provide help, organizers spend time and funds establishing and qualifying a new charitable organization. This may be appropriate when the organizers have long-term goals or where no suitable existing charity is present.

Alternatively, an existing charity operating in an allied area may be interested in establishing an assistance program for a particular disaster or emergency hardship situation. This may be a more practical approach than the establishment of a new charitable organization. For instance, a community fund like the United Way, a religious organization like the Salvation Army, or a relief organization like the Red Cross are all existing organizations which have provided targeted disaster relief and emergency hardship assistance in response to natural and civil disasters and other unforeseen emergencies. It is important to note that the **existing charity must be given full control and authority over the program.**

Establishing a New Charitable Organization

Generally, a new charitable organization with actual or anticipated annual gross receipts in excess of $5,000 must apply for and obtain recognition of tax-exempt status from the IRS. There are exceptions to this general rule. Churches, synagogues, temples, and mosques may, but are not required to, apply for tax-exempt status from the IRS.

An organization qualifies as an exempt charitable organization if it is organized and operated exclusively for charitable purposes, serves public rather than private interests, and refrains from participating or intervening in any political campaign or engaging in substantial amounts of lobbying activity. Use the following IRS materials when establishing a charitable organization:

When you use this factor:	You should consider these questions:
Publication 557, *Tax-Exempt Status for Your Organization*	Provides basic requirements to qualify as a tax-exempt, charitable organization, and describes the application process.
Form 1023, *Application for Recognition of Exemption from Federal Income Tax Under Section 501(c)(3) of the Internal Revenue Code*	Disaster and emergency hardship relief organizations may obtain expeditious handling of their Forms 1023. The request for expeditious treatment should be included in a cover letter accompanying the application, and should explain the circumstances justifying the request; for example, a brief description of the disaster and the reason for urgency in processing the application.

(continues)

(continued)

When you use this factor:	You should consider these questions:
Employer Identification Number (EIN)	Tax-exempt organizations must have an EIN that is used to identify the organization for filing and reporting purposes. You may obtain an EIN by:
	1. Filing Form SS-4, Application for Employer Identification Number, with the IRS. You may obtain Form SS-4 with instructions at:
	• www.irs.gov
	• (800) 829-3676 to order IRS tax forms and publications
	• (703) 368-9694 to dial IRS Tax Fax from a fax machine. Follow voice prompts to have forms faxed back to you.
	2. Calling Tele-TIN (Taxpayer Identification Number) program. The Tele-TIN phone numbers are included in the Form SS-4 instructions and are available by calling the Exempt Organizations IRS toll-free Customer Account Services at (877) 829-5500.

Publication 557, Tax Exempt Status for Your Organization

Provides basic requirements to qualify as a tax-exempt, charitable organization, and describes the application process.

Form 1023, Application for Recognition of Exemption from Federal Income Tax Under Section 501(c)(3) of the Internal Revenue Code

Disaster and emergency hardship relief organizations may obtain expeditious handling of their Forms 1023. The request for expeditious treatment should be included in a cover letter accompanying the application, and should explain the circumstances justifying the request; for example, a brief description of the disaster and the reason for urgency in processing the application.

Employer Identification Number (EIN)

Tax-exempt organizations must have an EIN that is used to identify the organization for filing and reporting purposes. You may obtain an EIN by:

1. Filing Form SS-4, Application for Employer Indentification Number, with the IRS. You may obtain Form SS-4 with instructions at:
   - www.irs.gov
   - (800) 829-3676 to order IRS tax forms and publications
2. Faxing Form SS-4 to a location provided in the instructions on the Form.
3. Calling (866) 816-2065 to get an EIN.
4. Calling (215) 516-6999 to obtain an EIN if you are located outside the United States.

Form 8718, User Fee for Exempt Organization Determination Letter Request

Form 8718 and the required User Fee must accompany the Form 1023, Application for Recognition of Exemption from Federal Income Tax Under Section 501(c)(3) of the Internal Revenue Code. The Form 1023 will not be processed without the necessary fee. Form 8718 is available by calling the IRS at (800) 829-3676 or downloading from *www.irs.gov.*

How Charitable Organizations Help Victims

The following sections describe how charitable organizations can provide assistance to disaster or emergency hardship victims in a variety of ways that accomplish charitable purposes.

AID TO INDIVIDUALS—Disaster relief or emergency hardship organizations may provide assistance in the form of funds, services, or goods to ensure that victims have the basic necessities, such as food, clothing, housing (including repairs), transportation, and medical assistance (including psychological counseling). The type of aid that is appropriate depends on the individual's needs and resources. For example, immediately following a devastating flood, a family may be in need of food, clothing, and shelter, regardless of their financial resources. However, they may not require long-term assistance if they have adequate financial resources.

Individuals who are financially needy or otherwise distressed are appropriate recipients of charity. Financial need and/or distress may arise through a variety of circumstances.

Examples include individuals who are:
- temporarily in need of food or shelter when stranded, injured, or lost because of a disaster
- temporarily unable to be self-sufficient as a result of a sudden and severe personal or family crisis, such as victims of crimes of violence or physical abuse
- in need of long-term assistance for housing, childcare, or educational expense because of a disaster
- in need of counseling because of trauma experienced as a result of a disaster or crime

AID TO BUSINESSES—Disaster assistance may also be provided to businesses to achieve the following charitable purposes:
- to aid individual business owners who are financially needy or otherwise
- distressed
- to combat community deterioration
- to lessen the burdens of government

CHARITABLE CLASS—The group of individuals that may properly receive assistance from a charitable organization is called a charitable class. A charitable class must be **large or indefinite** enough that providing aid to members of the class benefits the community as a whole. Because of this requirement, a tax-exempt disaster relief or emergency hardship organization cannot target and limit its assistance to specific individuals, such as a few persons injured in a particular fire. Similarly, donors cannot earmark contributions to a charitable organization for a particular individual or family. When a disaster or emergency hardship occurs, a charitable organization may help individuals who are needy or otherwise distressed because they are part of a general class of charitable beneficiaries, provided the organization selects who gets the assistance.

Example 1

Linda's baby, Todd, suffers a severe burn from a fire requiring costly treatment that Linda cannot afford. Linda's friends and co-workers form the Todd Foundation to raise funds from fellow workers, family members, and the general public to meet Todd's expenses. Since the organization is formed to assist a **particular individual,** it **would not qualify** as a charitable organization.

Consider this alternative case: Linda's friends and co-workers form an organization to raise funds to meet the expenses of an open-ended group consisting of all children in the community injured by disasters where financial help is needed. Neither Linda nor members of Linda's family control the charitable organization. The organization controls the selection of aid recipients and determines whether any assistance for Todd is appropriate. Potential donors are advised that, while funds may be used to assist Todd, their contributions might well be used for other children who have similar needs. The organization does not accept contributions specifically earmarked for Todd or any other individual. The organization, formed and operated to assist an **indefinite** number of persons, **qualifies** as a charitable organization.

See the example below in the section on gifts and charitable contribution rules for a situation where providing disaster assistance apart from a qualified charity is desirable.

Example 2

A hurricane causes widespread damage to property and loss of life in several counties of a coastal state. Over 100,000 homes are damaged or destroyed by high winds and floods. The **group of people affected** by the disaster **is large** enough so that providing aid to this group benefits the public as a whole. Therefore, a charitable organization can be formed to assist persons in this group since the eligible recipients comprise a charitable class.

Example 3

A hurricane causes widespread damage to property and loss of life in several counties of a coastal state. In one of the affected counties, an existing charitable organization has an ongoing program that provides emergency assistance to residents of the county. A small number of residents of this county suffered significant injury or property damage as a result of the storm. The organization provided assistance to some of these individuals. The organization's assistance was provided to a charitable class because the group of potential recipients is indefinite in that it is open-ended to include other victims of future disasters in the county.

NEEDY OR DISTRESSED TEST—Generally, a disaster relief or emergency hardship organization must make a specific assessment that a recipient of aid is financially or otherwise in need. Individuals do not have to be totally destitute to be financially needy; they may merely lack the resources to obtain basic necessities. Under established rules, charitable funds cannot be distributed to individuals merely because they are victims of a disaster. Therefore, an organization's decision about how its funds will be distributed must be based on an objective evaluation of the victim's needs at the time the grant is made. The scope of the assessment required to support the need for assistance may vary depending upon the circumstances.

A charity may provide crisis counseling, rescue services, or emergency aid such as blankets or hot meals without a showing of financial need. The individuals requiring these services are distressed irrespective of financial condition. In contrast, providing three to six months of financial assistance to families to pay for basic housing because of a disaster or emergency hardship would require a financial need assessment before disbursing aid.

An individual who is eligible for assistance because the individual is a victim of a disaster or emergency hardship has no automatic right to a charity's funds. For example, a charitable organization that provides disaster or emergency hardship relief does not have to make an individual whole, such as by rebuilding the individual's uninsured home destroyed by a flood, or replacing an individual's income after the person becomes unemployed as the result of a civil disturbance. This issue is especially relevant when the volume of contributions received in response to appeals exceeds the immediate needs. A charitable organization is responsible for taking into account the charitable purposes for which it was formed, the public benefit of its activities, and the specific needs and resources of each victim when using its discretion to distribute its funds.

SHORT-TERM AND LONG-TERM ASSISTANCE—Often charitable organizations (or programs by existing charities) are established as a result of a particular disaster where both short-term and long-term assistance might be required. The following types of assistance, if based on individual need, would be consistent with charitable purposes:

• assistance to allow a surviving spouse with young children to remain at home with the children to maintain the psychological well-being of the entire family

• assistance with elementary and secondary school tuition and higher education costs to permit a child to attend a school

• assistance with rent, mortgage payments, or car loans to prevent loss of a primary home or transportation that would cause additional trauma to families already suffering

• travel costs for family members to attend funerals and to provide comfort to survivors

Example

A group of individuals are killed in a fire in a large office complex. A charitable organization was previously formed to assist needy individuals in the surrounding region. The charity determines that some victims' spouses and dependents lack adequate resources to meet immediate basic needs; others have resources to meet these needs, but will likely have a continuing need for counseling, medical, housing, childcare, and education expenses. In this circumstance, the organization can grant funds to assist in meeting current and continuing needs.

The organization can also set aside funds for possible future needs. However, when payments are made out of the set-aside funds, they must be based on needs of victims' families that exist at the time the payments are made.

Documentation

An organization must maintain adequate records that demonstrate the victims' needs for the assistance provided. These records must also show that the organization's payments further charitable purposes. Thus, records are required when aid is provided to individuals based on a specific assessment of need, as described above, or under the special statutory rule for September 11, 2001, disaster relief that is described below. Documentation should include:

- a complete description of the assistance
- the purpose for which the aid was given
- the charity's objective criteria for disbursing assistance under each program
- how the recipients were selected
- the name, address, and amount distributed to each recipient
- any relationship between a recipient and officers, directors, or key employees of or substantial contributors to the charitable organization

A charitable organization that is distributing short-term emergency assistance would only be expected to maintain records such as the type of assistance pro-vided, criteria for disbursing assistance, date, place, estimated number of victims assisted (individual names and addresses are not required), charitable purpose intended to be accomplished, and the cost of the aid. Examples of such short-term emergency aid would include blankets, hot meals, electric fans, or coats, hats, and gloves. An organization that is distributing longer-term aid should keep the above more-detailed records.

Special Statutory Rule for September 11, 2001 Disaster Relief

In light of the extraordinary distress caused by the terrorist attacks on the United States of September 11, 2001, and the subsequent attacks involving anthrax, a special statutory rule was enacted by Congress to allow charitable organizations to disburse aid to victims of these attacks and their families without the charity making a specific assessment of need.

Under the Victims of Terrorism Tax Relief Act of 2001, charitable organizations making payments "by reason of the death, injury, wounding, or illness of an individual incurred as the result of the terrorist attacks against the United States on September 11, 2001, or an attack involving anthrax occurring on or after September 11, 2001, and before January 1, 2002," are not required to make a specific assessment of need as is the case under established rules. This special statutory rule for September 11 relief applies **provided that the organization makes the payments in good faith using a reasonable and objective formula which is consistently applied.** While a specific need assessment is not required, September 11 relief assistance must serve a charitable class that is large and/or indefinite in size.

In applying this special statutory rule the IRS will interpret:

- **good faith** to mean that the charity is applying its best efforts to accomplish its charitable purpose
- **a reasonable and objective formula that is consistently applied** to mean that the charity is using objective distribution criteria that take into account all pertinent circumstances, including the size of the amounts distributed, to avoid impermissible private benefit.

Thus, a charitable organization may distribute aid to a charitable class of September 11 and anthrax attack victims using a reasonable and objective formula that is applied consistently to all distributions. In that case, the charity does not have to take into account the specific needs of each recipient. Disaster relief payments made in accordance with this special statutory rule are treated as related to the organization's charitable purposes. Of course, charities may still choose to make needs assessments in determining assistance payments to September 11 and anthrax attack victims. The special statutory rule is an option, not a requirement.

APPLICATION OF THE SPECIAL STATUTORY RULE—Under the special rule, a charitable organization that assists families of victims killed in the line of duty as a result of the terrorist attacks of September 11, 2001, could make a distribution to families of the victims based on the number of families, family size, or the age of dependent children even though the specific financial and other needs of each family are not directly considered. By contrast, to distribute money based on the recipients' living expenses before September 11 would not be a reasonable formula under the special statutory rule because it could result in significantly greater assistance to individuals in a better position to provide for themselves than to individuals with fewer financial resources.

The following examples demonstrate application of the special rule.

Example 1

Families A, B, and C are members of a charitable class of families who lost a family member in the World Trade Center attack on September 11, 2001. Charity X distributes funds to each family based on a formula that provides a grant of $25,000 per immediate family member. Even though payments vary between families, because the formula is based on the number of family members, the method is considered both objective and reasonable in rationale. Charity X's distributions are treated as related to its charitable purposes under the special statutory rule.

Family Living Expenses	Current Living Expenses	Family Size	Payment ($25,000 per Member)
A	$500,000	5	$125,000
B	$100,000	4	$100,000
C	$ 25,000	4	$100,000

Example 2

Families A, B, and C are members of a charitable class who, lost a family member in the World Trade Center attack on September 11, 2001. Charity Y provides each family with a distribution based on 20% of their annual living expenses before September 11. While this formula is considered objective, it is not considered reasonable in its rationale because it could result in greater assistance to families who may be in a better position to provide for themselves. Charity Y's distributions are not treated as related to its charitable purposes under the special statutory rule.

Family Living Expenses	Prior Living Expenses	Family Size	Payment (20% of prior living expenses)
A	$500,000	5	$125,000
B	$100,000	4	$100,000
C	$ 25,000	4	$100,000

Note

Those charities providing assistance to September 11 and anthrax attack victims may use the special rule that allows for formula-based distributions with-out a specific need assessment. However, they do not have to use this rule when making payments. Charities can still make an assessment of need when making payments to victims, recognizing their unique circumstances. The following example shows the use of the special statutory rule plus a needs assessment which recognizes the unique circumstances of the victims.

Example 1

Families A, B, and C are members of a charitable class who lost an immediate family member in the World Trade Center attack of September 11, 2001. Charity Z decides it will distribute disaster relief aid based on both a distribution formula and a specific assessment of family needs. Charity Z makes a distribution of $10,000 to each surviving spouse and to each dependent child. In addition, the charity will assess the unique circumstances of each family member, including physical, emotional, and financial needs, and make additional distributions accordingly.

In this situation, Charity Z's proportionate distributions are treated as related to its charitable purposes under the special statutory rule. In addition, Charity Z's additional distributions based on a specific assessment of need are also consistent with accomplishing its charitable purposes.

The requirement for documentation, previously discussed, applies to assistance provided under the special statutory rule for September 11, 2001, disaster relief.

REPORTING—Most public charities and all private foundations are required to file an annual information return. A charity that makes payments using the special rule for September 11, 2001, disaster relief must specifically describe these payments in its annual return. Public charities filing Form 990, Return of Organization Exempt from Income Tax, must describe all such payments in a separate narrative of 'Program Service Accomplishments' on Part III of Form 990 or 990EZ. Private Foundations filing Form 990-PF, Return of Private Foundation, must describe all such payments in a separate narrative of 'Purpose of Grant or Contribution' in Part XV, Line 3, of Form 990-PF.

Employer-Sponsored Assistance Programs

Frequently, employers fund relief programs through charitable organizations aimed at assisting their employees in coping with personal tragedy. The types of benefits a charitable organization can provide through an employer-sponsored assistance program depend on whether the charity is a public charity or a private foundation.

Public charities generally receive broad public support; private foundations receive their funding or endowment from a limited number of sources. Because financial support from the general public typically carries with it public attention to and oversight of a charity's operations, federal tax laws allow public charities to provide a broader range of assistance to employees than can be provided by private foundations.

Publication 557, Tax-Exempt Status for your Organization, identifies distinctions between public charities and private foundations.

EMPLOYER-SPONSORED PRIVATE FOUNDATIONS—A private foundation that is employer-sponsored may make **qualified disaster** relief payments. A qualified disaster includes a disaster that results from certain terroristic or military actions, a Presidentially declared disaster, a disaster that results from an accident involving a common carrier or any other event that the Secretary of the Treasury determines is catastrophic.

The IRS will presume that **qualified disaster** payments made by a private foundation to employees (or their family members) of an employer that is a disqualified person (such as a company that is a substantial contributor) are consistent with the foundation's charitable purposes if:

- the class of beneficiaries is large or indefinite (a "charitable class"),
- the recipients are selected based on an objective determination of need, and
- the selection is made using either an independent selection committee or adequate substitute procedures to ensure that any benefit to the employer is incidental and tenuous. The foundation's selection committee is independent if a majority of the members of the committee consists of persons who are not in a position to exercise substantial influence over the affairs of the employer.

If the requirements of this presumption are met, then the foundation's payments in response to a qualified disaster (1) are treated as made for charitable purposes; (2) do not result in prohibited self-dealing merely because the recipient is an employee (or family member of an employee) of the employer-sponsor; and (3) do not result in taxable compensation to the employees.

This presumption is consistent with the legislative history accompanying the Victims of Terrorism Tax Relief Act of 2001 regarding the appropriate treatment of qualified disaster relief provided by private foundations controlled by a particular employer.

The presumption described above does not apply to payments that would otherwise constitute self-dealing. For example, the presumption does not apply to payments made to (or for the benefit of) individuals who are directors, officers, or trustees of the foundation. The presumption also does not apply to payments made to (or for the benefit of) individuals who are members of the foundation's selection committee.

Even though a private foundation fails to meet all the requirements of the presumption, the private foundation may still be operating consistent with the rules for charities when all the facts and circumstances are taken into account. Conversely, even though a private foundation meets the presumption, it can still be subject to review by the IRS of all the facts and circumstances to ensure that any benefit to the employer is tenuous and incidental. For example, a program may not be used to induce employees to follow a course of action sought by the employer or designed to relieve the employer of a legal obligation for employee benefits.

Example

A for-profit company is located in an area of the country designated a Presidentially declared disaster because of hurricane devastation. A private foundation funded by the company establishes a new program to provide assistance to the company's employees and their immediate family members who are victims of the current and any future qualified disasters.

The foundation's committee that selects recipients for assistance consists of a majority of members who are not in a position to exercise substantial influence over the affairs of the company. The foundation provides assistance to the employees and their families based on an objective determination of need.

(continues)

The foundation's program does not relieve the company of any legal obligation, such as an obligation under a collective bargaining agreement or a written plan that provides insurance benefits. The company does not use the program to recruit employees, to induce employees to continue their employment, or to otherwise follow a course of action sought by the company.

Because the foundation serves a charitable class, provides assistance based on an objective determination of need, and has an independent selection committee, the IRS will presume that it is carrying out a charitable program. Distributions are neither self-dealing transaction between the foundation and the employer nor taxable compensation to its employees under the program.

If the foundation also provides assistance to employees and their families who are victims of the September 11 attacks under the Victims of Terrorism Tax Relief Act of 2001, the foundation may distribute assistance to these victims without a specific assessment of need under the special rule described above.

Publication 578, Tax Information for Private Foundations and Foundation Managers, gives information about self-dealing and disqualified persons.

For a description of the types of records a private foundation must retain, see the previous section **Documentation.**

EMPLOYER-SPONSORED PUBLIC CHARITIES—Because public charities receive broad public support, they may establish employer-sponsored assistance programs to respond to any disaster or employee emergency hardship situations.

The IRS will presume that payments made by a public charity to employees (or their family members) for employer-sponsored disaster relief and emergency hardship are consistent with the charity's charitable purposes if:

- the class of beneficiaries is large or indefinite (a "charitable class"),

- the recipients are selected based on an objective determination of need, and

- the selection is made using either an independent selection committee or adequate substitute procedures to ensure that any benefit to the employer is incidental and tenuous. The charity's selection committee is independent if a majority of the members of the committee consists of persons who are not in a position to exercise substantial influence over the affairs of the employer.

If these requirements are met, the public charity's payments to employees (and their families) of the employer-sponsor, in response to a disaster or emergency hardship, are presumed: (1) to be made for charitable purposes, and (2) not to result in taxable compensation to the employees.

For a description of the types of records a public charity must retain, see the previous section **Documentation.**

Gifts and Charitable Contribution Rules

This part of the publication discusses the tax rules that apply to individuals who want to claim a tax deduction for their contributions to a qualified charitable organization. It also explains when gifts for disaster and emergency relief are not taxable income to recipients or subject to gift tax for contributors.

CHARITABLE CONTRIBUTIONS—Contributors to qualified, domestic charitable organizations may be eligible to claim federal income tax deductions for their contributions if they file itemized tax returns. Qualified organizations include charitable organizations that the IRS has determined are exempt from federal income tax. Domestic organizations are those created under the laws of the United States or its possessions. For charitable contribution purposes, United States possessions include Puerto Rico, the U.S. Virgin Islands, Guam, American Samoa, and the Commonwealth of Northern Mariana Islands. Churches, synagogues, temples, and mosques are also qualified charitable organizations.

See Publication 526, Charitable Contributions, for a complete description of qualified organizations.

Before making a contribution to an organization for disaster relief, a contributor may want to verify whether the contribution would be tax-deductible. A contributor may use any of the following means to determine if the organization is qualified to accept tax-deductible contributions:

- Call IRS Customer Service at (800) 829-1040
- Access Publication 78, Cumulative List of Organizations described in Section 170(c) of the Internal Revenue Code of 1986, for a list of qualified charitable organizations at www.irs.gov

Anyone may obtain a copy of an organization's exemption application or recent annual information returns, Form 990, Return of Organization Exempt from Income Tax, filed by most public charities with annual gross receipts in excess of $25,000, or Form 990-PF, Return of Private Foundation, filed by private foundations. A request for the organization's exemption application, Form 990 or Form 990-PF, can be made by contacting the organization directly or by submitting Form 4506-A, Request for Public Inspection or Copy of Exempt Organization IRS Form, to the IRS. Form 990 and Form 990-PF may also be posted on an organization's Web site.

When a contributor makes a contribution to a qualified charitable organiza- tion, the contributor must substantiate the amount of the contribution by maintaining reliable written records, such as cancelled checks or receipts. For more information about contributions, see Publication 526, Charitable Contributions.

For detailed information on what a charity is required to include in the writ- ten acknowledgement statements given to donors, see Publication 1771, Charitable Contributions —Substantiation and Disclosure Requirements.

FOREIGN CONTRIBUTIONS—Contributions to domestic, tax-exempt, chari- table organizations that provide assistance to individuals in foreign lands qualify as tax-deductible contributions for federal income tax purposes pro- vided the U.S. organization has full control and discretion over the uses of such funds. If the contributor is a corporation, its contributions for use in a foreign country are not deductible unless the domestic charity is itself organ- ized as a corporation for federal tax purposes.

Contributions to foreign organizations are generally not tax-deductible, unless permitted by a tax treaty. The United States currently has tax treaties with Canada, Mexico, and Israel. See Publication 526, Charitable Contributions, for limitations that apply pursuant to these treaties.

GIFTS—Individuals can also help victims of disaster or hardship by making gifts directly to victims. This type of assistance does not qualify as a tax- deductible contribution since a qualified charitable organization is not the recipient. However, individual recipients of gifts are generally not subject to federal income tax on the value of the gift. If you make a gift directly to an individual, you are not subject to federal gift tax unless the total gifts made in a year exceeds the annual exclusion.

Sometimes providing financial assistance apart from a qualified charity is desirable.

Example

Jim, a college student and a counselor at a summer camp, accidentally rolls his old truck into a lake. The other counselors collect several hundred dollars and give the monies directly to Jim to help with the down payment for another truck. Since the counselors are making gifts to a particular individual, the use of a qualified charitable organization would not be appropriate. The counselors cannot claim tax deductions for their gifts to Jim. However, Jim is not subject to federal income tax on the gift amount. The other counselors would not be subject to federal gift tax if the total gifts made by each counselor to Jim during the year did not exceed the annual exclusion amount.

For more information about the taxability of gifts, see Publication 950, Introduction to Estate and Gift Taxes. You can download IRS publications at www.irs.gov or order free copies from the IRS at (800) 829-3676.

Additional Help on Disaster-Related Topics

The IRS has a number of forms and publications on disaster relief that may be helpful to your organization.

FORMS AND PUBLICATIONS—To order free IRS publications and forms, call the IRS at (800) 829-3676. Download IRS publications and forms at www.irs.gov.

Form 1023	*Application for Recognition of Exemption Under Section 501(c)(3) of the Internal Revenue Code*
Form 8718	*User Fee for Exempt Organization Determination Letter Request*
Publication 526	*Charitable Contributions*
Publication 547	*Casualties, Disasters and Thefts (Business and Non-Business)*
Publication 557	*Tax-Exempt Status for Your Organization*
Publication 578	*Tax Information for Private Foundations and Foundation Managers*

(continues)

Publication 950	*Introduction to Estate and Gift Taxes*
Publication 1600	*Disaster Losses—Help From the IRS*
Publication 1771	*Charitable Contributions—Substantiation and Disclosure Requirements*
Publication 2194	*Disaster Assistance Kit*

TELEPHONE ASSISTANCE—The following telephone numbers will connect you to IRS Customer Service.

(877) 829-5500	IRS Exempt Organizations Customer Account Services for tax information specific to exempt organizations
(202) 874-1460	IRS Foreign Assistance Customer Service for tax information specific to foreign tax issues
(800) 829-1040	IRS Customer Service for general tax information

Appendix E

IRS Publication 526—
Charitable Contributions
(Rev. December 2000) Cat. No. 15050A

Introduction

This publication explains how to claim a deduction for your charitable contributions. It discusses organizations that are qualified to receive deductible charitable contributions, the types of contributions you can deduct, how much you can deduct, what records to keep, and how to report charitable contributions.

A **charitable contribution** is a donation or gift to, or for the use of, a **qualified organization.** It is voluntary and is made without getting, or expecting to get, anything of equal value.

Qualified organizations. Qualified organizations include nonprofit groups that are religious, charitable, educational, scientific, or literary in purpose, or that work to prevent cruelty to children or animals. You will find descriptions of these organizations under *Organizations That Qualify to Receive Deductible Contributions.*

Form 1040 required. To deduct a charitable contribution, you must file Form 1040 and itemize deductions on Schedule A. The amount of your deduction may be limited if certain rules and limits explained in this publication apply to you.

Comments and suggestions. We welcome your comments about this publication and your suggestions for future editions.

You can e-mail us while visiting our website at **www.irs.gov/help/email2.html.**

You can write to us at the following address:

Internal Revenue Service
Technical Publications Branch
W:CAR:MP:FP:P
1111 Constitution Ave. NW
Washington, DC 20224

We respond to many letters by telephone. Therefore, it would be helpful if you would include your daytime phone number, including the area code, in your correspondence.

Useful Items

You may want to see:

Publication

- **78** Cumulative List of Organizations
- **561** Determining the Value of Donated Property

Form (and Instructions)

- **Schedule A (Form 1040)** Itemized Deductions
- **8283** Noncash Charitable Contributions

See *How To Get Tax Help* near the end of this publication for information about getting these publications and forms.

Organizations that Qualify to Receive Deductible Contributions

You can deduct your contributions only if you make them to a *qualified organization*. To become a **qualified organization,** most organizations other than churches and governments, as described below, must apply to the IRS.

Publication 78. You can ask any organization whether it is a qualified organization, and most will be able to tell you. Or you can check IRS Publication 78, which lists most qualified organizations. You may find

Publication 78 in your local library's reference section. If not, you can call the IRS to find out if an organization is qualified. Call **1-800-829-1040.** (For TTY/TDD help, call **1-800-829-4059.**)

Types of Qualified Organizations

Generally, only the five following types of organizations can be qualified organizations.

1. **A community chest, corporation, trust, fund, or foundation** organized or created in or under the laws of the United States, any state, the District of Columbia, or any possession of the United States (including Puerto Rico). It must be organized and operated only for one or more of the following purposes:

   a. Religious

   b. Charitable

   c. Educational

   d. Scientific

   e. Literary

   f. The prevention of cruelty to children or animals

   Certain organizations that foster national or international amateur sports competition also qualify.

2. **War veterans' organizations,** including posts, auxiliaries, trusts, or foundations, organized in the United States or any of its possessions.

3. **Domestic fraternal societies,** orders, and associations operating under the lodge system.

   Note. Your contribution to this type of organization is deductible only if it is to be used solely for charitable, religious, scientific, literary, or educational purposes, or for the prevention of cruelty to children or animals.

4. **Certain nonprofit cemetery companies** or corporations.

   Note. Your contribution to this type of organization is not deductible if it can be used for the care of a specific lot or mausoleum crypt.

5. **The United States** or any state, the District of Columbia, a U.S. possession (including Puerto Rico), a political subdivision of a state or U.S. possession, or an Indian tribal government or any of its subdivisions that perform substantial government functions.

Note. To be deductible, your contribution to this type of organization must be made solely for public purposes.

Example 1. You contribute cash to your city's police department to be used as a reward for information about a crime. The city police department is a qualified organization, and your contribution is for a public purpose. You can deduct your contribution.

Example 2. You make a voluntary contribution to the social security trust fund, not earmarked for a specific account. Because the trust fund is part of the U.S. Government, you contributed to a qualified organization. You can deduct your contribution.

Examples. The following lists gives some examples of qualified organizations.

- Churches, a convention or association of churches, temples, synagogues, mosques, and other religious organizations.
- Most nonprofit charitable organizations such as the Red Cross and the United Way.
- Most nonprofit educational organizations, including the Girl (and Boy) Scouts of America, colleges, museums, and day-care centers if substantially all the child care provided is to enable individuals (the parents) to be gainfully employed and the services are available to the general public. However, if your contribution is a substitute for tuition or other enrollment fee, it is not deductible as a charitable contribution, as explained later under *Contributions You Cannot Deduct.*
- Nonprofit hospitals and medical research organizations.
- Utility company emergency energy programs, if the utility company is an agent for a charitable organization that assists individuals with emergency energy needs.
- Nonprofit volunteer fire companies.
- Public parks and recreation facilities.
- Civil defense organizations.

Canadian charities. You may be able to deduct contributions to certain Canadian charitable organizations covered under an income tax treaty with Canada.

To deduct your contribution to a Canadian charity, you generally must have income from sources in Canada. See Publication 597, *Information on the United States–Canada Income Tax Treaty*, for information on how to figure your deduction.

Mexican charities. You may be able to deduct contributions to certain Mexican charitable organizations under an income tax treaty with Mexico.

The organization must meet tests that are essentially the same as the tests that qualify U.S. organizations to receive deductible contributions. The organization may be able to tell you if it meets these tests.

> *Mail*
>
> If not, you can get general information about the tests the organization must meet by writing to the:
>
> > Internal Revenue Service
> > International Returns Section
> > P.O. Box 920
> > Bensalem, PA 19020-8518

To deduct your contribution to a Mexican charity, you must have income from sources in Mexico. The limits described in *Limits on Deductions*, later, apply and are figured using your income from Mexican sources. Those limits also apply to all your charitable contributions, as described in that discussion.

Israeli charities. You may be able to deduct contributions to certain Israeli charitable organizations under an income tax treaty with Israel. To qualify for the deduction, your contribution must be made to an organization created and recognized as a charitable organization under the laws of Israel. The deduction will be allowed in the amount that would be allowed if the organization was created under the laws of the United States, but is limited to 25% of your adjusted gross income from Israeli sources.

Contributions You Can Deduct

Generally, you can deduct your contributions of money or property that you make to, or for the use of, a qualified organization. A gift or contribution is "for the use of" a qualified organization when it is held in a legally enforceable trust for the qualified organization or in a similar legal arrangement.

The contributions must be made to a qualified organization and not set aside for use by a specific person.

If you give property to a qualified organization, you generally can deduct the fair market value of the property at the time of the contribution. See *Contributions of Property*, later.

Your deduction for charitable contributions is generally limited to 50% of your adjusted gross income, but in some cases 20% and 30% limits may apply. See *Limits on Deductions*, later.

The total of your charitable contributions deduction and certain other itemized deductions may be limited. See the instructions for Form 1040 for more information.

Table E.1 in this publication lists some examples of contributions you can deduct and some that you cannot deduct.

Contributions from which You Benefit

If you receive a benefit as a result of making a contribution to a qualified organization, you can deduct only the amount of your contribution that is **more than the value of the benefit** you receive. Also see *Contributions from which You Benefit* under *Contributions You Cannot Deduct*, later.

If you pay more than fair market value to a qualified organization for merchandise, goods, or services, the amount you pay that is more than the value of the item can be a charitable contribution. For the excess amount to qualify, you must pay it with the intent to make a charitable contribution.

Example 1. You pay $65 for a ticket to a dinner-dance at a church. All the proceeds of the function go to the church. The ticket to the dinner-dance has a fair market value of $25. When you buy your ticket, you know that its value is less than your payment. To figure the amount of your charitable contribution, you subtract the value of the benefit you receive ($25) from your

Table E.1 *Examples of Charitable Contributions—A Quick Check*

Use the following lists for a quick check of contributions you can or cannot deduct. See the rest of this publication for more information and additional rules and limits that may apply.

Deductible As Charitable Contributions	Not Deductible As Charitable Contributions
Money or property you give to:	Money or property you give to:
• Churches, synagogues, temples, mosques, and other religious organizations	• Civic leagues, social and sports clubs, labor unions, and chambers of commerce
• Federal, state, and local governments, if your contribution is solely for public purposes (for example, a gift to reduce the public debt)	• Foreign organizations (except certain Canadian, Israeli, and Mexican charities)
• Nonprofit schools and hospitals	• Groups that are run for personal profit
• Public parks and recreation facilities	• Groups whose purpose is to lobby for law changes
• Salvation Army, Red Cross, CARE, Goodwill Industries, United Way, Boy Scouts, Girl Scouts, Boys and Girls Clubs of America, etc.	• Homeowners' associations
	• Individuals
• War veterans' groups	• Political groups or candidates for public office
Expenses paid for a student living with you, sponsored by a qualified organization	Cost of raffle, bingo, or lottery tickets
Out-of-pocket expenses when you serve a qualified organization as a volunteer	Dues, fees, or bills paid to country clubs, lodges, fraternal orders, or similar groups
	Tuition
	Value of your time or services
	Value of blood given to a blood bank

total payment ($65). You can deduct $40 as a charitable contribution to the church.

Example 2. At a fund-raising auction conducted by a charity, you pay $600 for a week's stay at a beach house. The amount you pay is no more than the fair rental value. You have not made a deductible charitable contribution.

Athletic events. If you make a payment to, or for the benefit of, a college or university and, as a result, you receive the right to buy tickets to an athletic event in the athletic stadium of the college or university, you can deduct 80% of the payment as a charitable contribution.

If any part of your payment is for tickets (rather than the right to buy tickets), that part is not deductible. In that case, subtract the price of the tickets from your payment. 80% of the remaining amount is a charitable contribution.

Example 1. You pay $300 a year for membership in an athletic scholarship program maintained by a university (a qualified organization). The only benefit of membership is that you have the right to buy one season ticket for a seat in a designated area of the stadium at the university's home football games. You can deduct $240 (80% of $300) as a charitable contribution.

Example 2. The facts are the same as in *Example 1* except that your $300 payment included the purchase of one season ticket for the stated ticket price of $120. You must subtract the usual price of a ticket ($120) from your $300 payment. The result is $180. Your deductible charitable contribution is $144 (80% of $180).

Charity benefit events. If you pay a qualified organization more than fair market value for the right to attend a charity ball, banquet, show, sporting event, or other benefit event, you can deduct only the amount that is more than the value of the privileges or other benefits you receive.

If there is an established charge for the event, that charge is the value of your benefit. If there is no established charge, your contribution is that part of your payment that is more than the reasonable value of the right to attend the event. Whether you use the tickets or other privileges has no effect on the amount you can deduct. However, if you return the ticket to the qualified organization for resale, you can deduct the entire amount you paid for the ticket.

Caution
Even if the ticket or other evidence of payment indicates that the payment is a "contribution," this does not mean you can deduct the entire amount. If the ticket shows the price of admission and the amount of the contribution, you can deduct the contribution amount.

Example. You pay $40 to see a special showing of a movie for the benefit of a qualified organization. Printed on the ticket is "Contribution— $40." If the regular price for the movie is $8, your contribution is $32 ($40 payment – $8 regular price).

Membership fees or dues. You may be able to deduct membership fees or dues you pay to a qualified organization. However, you can deduct only the amount that is more than the value of the benefits you receive. You cannot deduct dues, fees, or assessments paid to country clubs and other social organizations. They are not qualified organizations.

Certain membership benefits can be disregarded. Both you and the organization can disregard certain membership benefits you get in return for an annual payment of **$75 or less** to the qualified organization. You can pay more than $75 to the organization if the organization does not require a larger payment for you to get the benefits. The benefits covered under this rule are:

1. Any rights or privileges, other than those discussed under *Athletic events*, earlier, that you can use frequently while you are a member, such as:
   a. Free or discounted admission to the organization's facilities or events,
   b. Free or discounted parking,
   c. Preferred access to goods or services, and
   d. Discounts on the purchase of goods and services, and
2. Admission, while you are a member, to events that are open only to members of the organization if the organization reasonably projects that the cost per person (excluding any allocated overhead) is not more than a specified amount, which may be adjusted annually for inflation. (This is the amount for low-cost articles given in the annual revenue procedure with inflation adjusted amounts for the current year. You can get this figure from the IRS.)

Token items. You can deduct your entire payment to a qualified organization as a charitable contribution if both of the following are true.

1. You get a small item or other benefit of token value.
2. The qualified organization correctly determines that the value of the item or benefit you received is not substantial and informs you that you can deduct your payment in full.

The organization determines whether the value of an item or benefit is substantial by using Revenue Procedure 90-12 and 92-49 and the revenue procedure with the inflation adjusted amounts for the current year.

Written statement. A qualified organization must give you a written statement if you make a payment to it that is **more than $75** and is partly a contribution and partly for goods or services. The statement must tell you that you can deduct only the amount of your payment that is more than the value of the goods or services you received. It must also give you a good faith estimate of the value of those goods or services.

The organization can give you the statement either when it solicits or when it receives the payment from you.

Exception. An organization will not have to give you this statement if one of the following is true.

1. The organization is:
    a. The type of organization described in (5) under *Types of Qualified Organizations*, earlier, or
    b. Formed only for religious purposes, and the only benefit you receive is an intangible religious benefit (such as admission to a religious ceremony) that generally is not sold in commercial transactions outside the donative context.
2. You receive only items whose value is not substantial as described under *Token items*, earlier.
3. You receive only membership benefits that can be disregarded, as described earlier.

Expenses Paid for Student Living with You

You may be able to deduct some expenses of having a student live with you. You can deduct **qualifying expenses** for a foreign or American student who:

1. Lives in your home under a written agreement between you and a **qualified organization** (defined later) as part of a program of the organization to provide educational opportunities for the student,

2. Is not your dependent or relative, and

3. Is a full-time student in the twelfth or any lower grade at a school in the United States.

> **Tip**
> You can deduct up to $50 a month for each full calendar month the student lives with you. Any month when conditions (1) through (3) above are met for 15 or more days counts as a full month.

Qualified organization. For these purposes, a qualified organization can be any of the organizations described earlier under *Organizations That Qualify To Receive Deductible Contributions,* except those in (4) and (5). For example, if you are providing a home for a student through a state or local government agency, you cannot deduct your expenses as charitable contributions.

Qualifying expenses. Expenses that you may be able to deduct include the cost of books, tuition, food, clothing, transportation, medical and dental care, entertainment, and other amounts you actually spend for the well-being of the student.

Expenses that do not qualify. Depreciation on your home, the fair market value of lodging, and similar items are not considered amounts spent by you. In addition, general household expenses, such as taxes, insurance, repairs, etc., do not qualify for the deduction.

Reimbursed expenses. If you are compensated or reimbursed for any part of the costs of having a student living with you, you cannot deduct **any** of your costs. However, if you are reimbursed for only an extraordinary or a one-time item, such as a hospital bill or vacation trip, that you paid in advance at the request of the student's parents or the sponsoring organization, you can deduct your expenses for the student for which you were not reimbursed.

Mutual exchange program. You cannot deduct the costs of a foreign student living in your home under a mutual exchange program through which your child will live with a family in a foreign country.

Reporting expenses. For a list of what you must file with your return if you deduct expenses for a student living with you, see *Reporting expenses for student living with you under How To Report,* later.

Out-of-Pocket Expenses in Giving Services

You may be able to deduct some amounts you pay in giving services to a qualified organization. The amounts must be:

• Unreimbursed,

• Directly connected with the services,

• Expenses you had only because of the services you gave, and

• Not personal, living, or family expenses.

Table E.2 contains questions and answers that apply to some individuals who volunteer their services.

Underprivileged youths selected by charity. You can deduct reasonable unreimbursed out-of-pocket expenses you pay to allow underprivileged youths to attend athletic events, movies, or dinners. The youths must be selected by a charitable organization whose goal is to reduce juvenile delinquency. Your own similar expenses in accompanying the youths are not deductible.

Conventions. If you are a chosen representative attending a convention of a qualified organization, you can deduct unreimbursed expenses for travel and transportation, including a reasonable amount for meals and lodging, while away from home overnight in connection with the convention. However, see *Travel,* later.

You cannot deduct personal expenses for sightseeing, fishing parties, theater tickets, or nightclubs. You also cannot deduct travel, meals and lodging, and other expenses for your spouse or children.

You cannot deduct your expenses in attending a church convention if you go only as a member of your church rather than as a chosen representative. You can deduct unreimbursed expenses that are directly connected with giving services for your church during the convention.

Table E.2 *Volunteers' Questions and Answers*

If you do volunteer work for a **qualified organization,** the following questions and answers may apply to you. All of the rules explained in this publication also apply. See, in particular, *Out-of-Pocket Expenses in Giving Services.*

Question	Answer
I do volunteer work 6 hours a week in the office of a qualified organization. The receptionist is paid $6 an hour to do the same work I do. Can I deduct $36 a week for my time?	No, you cannot deduct the value of your time or services.
The office is 30 miles from my home. Can I deduct any of my car expenses for these trips?	Yes, you can deduct the costs of gas and oil that are directly related to getting to and from the place where you are a volunteer. If you do not want to figure your actual costs, you can use the standard mileage rate. See the instructions for Schedule A (Form 1040) for this rate.
I volunteer as a Red Cross nurse's aide at a hospital. Can I deduct the cost of uniforms that I must wear?	Yes, you can deduct the cost of buying and cleaning your uniforms if the hospital is a qualified organization, the uniforms are not suitable for everyday use, and you must wear them when volunteering.
I pay a baby sitter to watch my children while I do volunteer work for a qualified organization. Can I deduct these costs?	No, you cannot deduct payments for child care expenses as a charitable contribution, even if they are necessary so you can do volunteer work for a qualified organization. (If you have child care expenses so you can work for pay, get Publication 503, *Child and Dependent Care Expenses.*)

Uniforms. You can deduct the cost and upkeep of uniforms that are not suitable for everyday use and that you must wear while performing donated services for a charitable organization.

Foster parents. You may be able to deduct as a charitable contribution some of the costs of being a foster parent (foster care provider) if you have no profit motive in providing the foster care and are not, in fact, making a profit. A qualified organization must designate the individuals you take into your home for foster care.

You can deduct expenses that meet both of the following requirements.
1. They are unreimbursed out-of-pocket expenses to feed, clothe, and care for the foster child.
2. They must be mainly to benefit the qualified organization.

Unreimbursed expenses that you cannot deduct as charitable contributions may be considered support provided by you in determining whether you can claim the foster child as a dependent. For details, see Publication 501, *Exemptions, Standard Deduction, and Filing Information.*

   Example. You cared for a foster child because you wanted to adopt her, not to benefit the agency that placed her in your home. Your unreimbursed expenses are not deductible as charitable contributions.

Church deacon. You can deduct as a charitable contribution any unreimbursed expenses you have while in a permanent diaconate program established by your church. These expenses include the cost of vestments, books, and transportation required in order to serve in the program as either a deacon candidate or as an ordained deacon.

Car expenses. You can deduct unreimbursed out-of-pocket expenses, such as the cost of gas and oil, that are directly related to the use of your car in giving services to a charitable organization. You cannot deduct general repair and maintenance expenses, depreciation, registration fees, or the costs of tires or insurance.

If you do not want to deduct your actual expenses, you can use a standard mileage rate to figure your contribution. See the instructions for Schedule A (Form 1040) to find the rate for the year you claim the deduction.

You can deduct parking fees and tolls, whether you use your actual expenses or the standard mileage rate.

You must keep reliable written records of your car expenses. For more information, see *Car expenses* under *Records To Keep,* later.

Travel. Generally, you can claim a charitable contribution deduction for travel expenses necessarily incurred while you are away from home performing services for a charitable organization only if there is *no significant element of personal pleasure,* recreation, or vacation in the travel. This applies whether you pay the expenses directly or indirectly. You are paying the expenses indirectly if you make a payment to the charitable organization and the organization pays for your travel expenses.

The deduction for travel expenses will not be denied simply because you enjoy providing services to the charitable organization. Even if you enjoy the trip, you can take a charitable contribution deduction for your travel expenses if you are on duty in a genuine and substantial sense throughout the trip. However, if you have only nominal duties, or if for significant parts of the trip you do not have any duties, you cannot deduct your travel expenses.

Example 1. You are a troop leader for a tax-exempt youth group and take the group on a camping trip. You are responsible for overseeing the set up of the camp and for providing the adult supervision for other activities during the entire trip. You participate in the activities of the group and really enjoy your time with them. You oversee the breaking of camp and you transport the group home. You can deduct your travel expenses.

Example 2. You sail from one island to another and spend 8 hours a day counting whales and other forms of marine life. The project is sponsored by a charitable organization. In most circumstances, you cannot deduct your expenses.

Example 3. You work for several hours each morning on an archeological dig sponsored by a charitable organization. The rest of the day is free for recreation and sightseeing. You cannot take a charitable contribution deduction even though you work very hard during those few hours.

Example 4. You spend the entire day attending a charitable organization's regional meeting as a chosen representative. In the evening you go to the theater. You can claim your travel expenses as charitable contributions, but you cannot claim the cost of your evening at the theater.

Daily allowance (per diem). If you provide services for a charitable organization and receive a daily allowance to cover reasonable travel expenses, including meals and lodging while away from home overnight, you must include in income the amount of the allowance that is more than your deductible travel expenses. You can deduct your necessary travel expenses that are more than the allowance.

Deductible travel expenses. These include:

- Air, rail, and bus transportation,
- Out-of-pocket expenses for your car,
- Taxi fares or other costs of transportation between the airport or station and your hotel,
- Lodging costs, and
- The cost of meals.

Because these travel expenses are not business-related, they are not subject to the same limits as business related expenses. For information on business travel expenses, see *Travel Expenses in Publication 463, Travel, Entertainment, Gift, and Car Expenses.*

Contributions You Cannot Deduct

There are some contributions that you cannot deduct. There are others that you can deduct only part of.

You cannot deduct as a charitable contribution:

1. A contribution to a specific **individual,**
2. A contribution to a **nonqualified organization,**
3. The part of a contribution from which you receive or expect to **receive a benefit,**
4. The **value of your time or services,**
5. Your **personal expenses,**
6. **Appraisal fees,** or
7. Certain contributions of **partial interests in property.**

Detailed discussions of these items follow.

Contributions to Individuals

You cannot deduct contributions to specific individuals, including:

- Contributions to fraternal societies made for the purpose of paying medical or burial expenses of deceased members.

- Contributions to individuals who are needy or worthy. This includes contributions to a qualified organization if you indicate that your contribution is for a specific person. But you can deduct a contribution that you give to a qualified organization that in turn helps needy or worthy individuals if you do not indicate that your contribution is for a specific person.

  Example. You can deduct contributions earmarked for flood relief, hurricane relief, or other disaster relief to a qualified organization. However, you cannot deduct contributions earmarked for relief of a particular individual or family.

- Payments to a member of the clergy that can be spent as he or she wishes, such as for personal expenses.

- Expenses you paid for another person who provided services to a qualified organization.

  Example. Your son does missionary work. You pay his expenses. You cannot claim a deduction for your son's unreimbursed expenses related to his contribution of services.

- Payments to a hospital that are for a specific patient's care or for services for a specific patient. You cannot deduct these payments even if the hospital is operated by a city, state, or other qualified organization.

Contributions to Nonqualified Organizations

You cannot deduct contributions to organizations that are not qualified to receive tax-deductible contributions, including the following organizations.

1. **Certain state bar associations** if:
   a. The state bar is not a political subdivision of a state,
   b. The bar has private, as well as public, purposes, such as promoting the professional interests of members, and
   c. Your contribution is unrestricted and can be used for private purposes.
2. **Chambers of commerce** and other business leagues or organizations.
3. **Civic leagues and associations.**

4. **Communist organizations.**

5. **Country clubs** and other social clubs.

6. **Foreign organizations** other than:

   a. A U.S. organization that transfers funds to a charitable foreign organization if the U.S. organization controls the use of the funds or if the foreign organization is only an administrative arm of the U.S. organization, or

   b. Certain Canadian, Israeli, or Mexican charitable organizations. See *Canadian charities, Mexican charities,* and *Israeli charities* under *Organizations That Qualify To Receive Deductible Contributions,* earlier.

7. **Homeowners' associations.**

8. **Labor unions.** But you may be able to deduct union dues as a miscellaneous itemized deduction, subject to the 2%-of-adjusted-gross-income limit, on Schedule A (Form 1040). See Publication 529, *Miscellaneous Deductions.*

9. **Political organizations and candidates.**

Contributions from which You Benefit

If you receive or expect to receive a financial economic benefit as a result of making a contribution to a qualified organization, you cannot deduct the part of the contribution that represents the value of the benefit you receive. See *Contributions from which You Benefit* under *Contributions You Can Deduct,* earlier. These contributions include:

- Contributions for **lobbying.** This includes amounts that you earmark for use in, or in connection with, influencing specific legislation.

- Contributions to a **retirement home** that are clearly for room, board, maintenance, or admittance. Also, if the amount of your contribution depends on the type or size of apartment you will occupy, it is not a charitable contribution.

- Costs of **raffles, bingo, lottery, etc.** You cannot deduct as a charitable contribution amounts you pay to buy raffle or lottery tickets or to play bingo or other games of chance. For information on how to report gambling winnings and losses, see *Deductions Not Subject to the 2% Limit* in Publication 529.

- Dues to **fraternal orders** and similar groups. However, see *Membership fees or dues* under *Contributions from which You Benefit,* earlier.

- **Tuition,** or amounts you pay instead of tuition, even if you pay them for children to attend parochial schools or qualifying nonprofit day-care centers. You also cannot deduct any fixed amount you may be required to pay in addition to the tuition fee to enroll in a private school, even if it is designated as a "donation."

- **Contributions connected with split-dollar insurance arrangements.** You cannot deduct any part of a contribution to a charitable organization if, in connection with the contribution, the organization directly or indirectly pays, has paid, or is expected to pay any premium on any life insurance, annuity, or endowment contract for which you, any member of your family or any other person chosen, you (other than a qualified charitable organization) is a beneficiary.

   Example. You donate money to a charitable organization. The charity uses the money to purchase a cash value life insurance policy. The beneficiaries under the insurance policy include members of your family. Even though the charity may eventually get some benefit out of the insurance policy, you cannot deduct any part of the donation.

Value of Time or Services

You cannot deduct the value of your time or services, including:

- **Blood donations** to the Red Cross or to blood banks, and
- **The value of income lost** while you work as an unpaid volunteer for a qualified organization.

Personal Expenses

You cannot deduct personal, living, or family expenses, such as the following items.

- **The cost of meals** you eat while you perform services for a qualified organization, unless it is necessary for you to be away from home overnight while performing the services.

- **Adoption expenses,** including fees paid to an adoption agency and the costs of keeping a child in your home before adoption is final. However, you may be able to claim a tax credit for these expenses. Also, you may be able to exclude from your gross income amounts paid or reimbursed by your employer for your adoption expenses. See Publication 968, *Tax Benefits for Adoption*, for more information. You also may be able to claim an exemption for the child. See *Adoption* in Publication 501 for more information.

Appraisal Fees

Fees that you pay to find the fair market value of donated property are not deductible as contributions. You can claim them, subject to the 2%-of-adjusted-gross-income limit, as a miscellaneous itemized deduction on Schedule A (Form 1040). See *Deductions Subject to the 2% Limit* in Publication 529 for more information.

Partial Interest in Property

Generally, you cannot deduct a contribution of less than your entire interest in property. For details, see *Partial interest in property* under *Contributions of Property*, later.

Contributions of Property

If you contribute property to a qualified organization, the amount of your charitable contribution is generally the **fair market value** of the property at the time of the contribution. However, if the property has increased in value, you may have to make some adjustments to the amount of your deduction. See *Giving Property That Has Increased in Value*, later.

For information about the records you must keep and the information you must furnish with your return if you donate property, see *Records To Keep* and *How To Report*, later.

Contributions Subject to Special Rules

Special rules apply if you contributed:
- Property subject to a debt,
- A partial interest in property,
- A future interest in tangible personal property, or
- Inventory from your business.

These special rules are described next.

Property subject to a debt. If you contribute property subject to a debt (such as a mortgage), you must reduce the fair market value of the property by:
  1. Any allowable deduction for interest that you paid (or will pay) attributable to any period after the contribution, and

2. If the property is a bond, the lesser of:

   a. Any allowable deduction for interest you paid (or will pay) to buy or carry the bond that is attributable to any period before the contribution, or

   b. The interest, including bond discount, receivable on the bond that is attributable to any period before the contribution, and that is not includible in your income due to your accounting method.

This prevents a double deduction of the same amount as investment interest and also as a charitable contribution.

If the debt is assumed by the recipient (or another person), you must also reduce the fair market value of the property by the amount of the outstanding debt.

If you sold the property to a qualified organization at a bargain price, the amount of the debt is also treated as an amount realized on the sale or exchange of property. For more information, see *Bargain Sales* under *Giving Property That Has Increased in Value*, later.

Partial interest in property. Generally, you cannot deduct a charitable contribution (not made by a transfer in trust) of less than your entire interest in property. A contribution of the right to use property is a contribution of less than your entire interest in that property and is not deductible.

   Example 1. You own a 10-story office building and donate rent-free use of the top floor to a charitable organization. Since you still own the building, you have contributed a partial interest in the property and cannot take a deduction for the contribution.

   Example 2. Mandy White owns a vacation home at the beach that she sometimes rents to others. For a fund-raising auction at her church, she donated the right to use the vacation home for one week. At the auction, the church received and accepted a bid from Lauren Green equal to the fair rental value of the home for one week. Mandy cannot claim a deduction because of the partial interest rule just discussed.

   Note. Lauren cannot claim a deduction either because she received a benefit equal to the amount of her payment. See *Contributions from which You Benefit*, earlier.

Exceptions. You can deduct a charitable contribution of a partial interest in property only if that interest represents one of the following listed items.

1. A remainder interest in your personal home or farm. A remainder interest is one that passes to a beneficiary after the end of an earlier interest in the property.

    Example. You keep the right to live in your home during your lifetime and give your church a remainder interest that begins upon your death.

2. An undivided part of your entire interest. This must consist of a part of every substantial interest or right you own in the property and must last as long as your interest in the property lasts.

    Example. You contribute voting stock to a qualified organization but keep the right to vote the stock. The right to vote is a substantial right in the stock. You have not contributed an undivided part of your entire interest and cannot deduct your contribution.

3. A partial interest that would be deductible if transferred in trust.

4. A qualified conservation contribution (defined under *Qualified conservation contribution* in Publication 561).

For information about how to figure the value of a contribution of a partial interest in property, see *Partial Interest in Property Not in Trust* in Publication 561.

Future interest in tangible personal property. You can deduct the value of a charitable contribution of a future interest in tangible personal property only after all intervening interests in and rights to the actual possession or enjoyment of the property have either expired or been turned over to someone other than yourself, a related person, or a related organization.

Related persons include your spouse, children, grandchildren, brothers, sisters, and parents. Related organizations may include a partnership or corporation that you have an interest in, or an estate or trust that you have a connection with.

Tangible personal property. This is any property, other than land or buildings, that can be seen or touched. It includes furniture, books, jewelry, paintings, and cars.

Future interest. This is any interest that is to begin at some future time, regardless of whether it is designated as a future interest under state law.

Example. You own an antique car that you contribute to a museum. You give up ownership, but retain the right to keep the car in your garage with your personal collection. Since you keep an interest in the property, you cannot deduct the contribution. If you turn the car over to the museum in a later year, giving up all rights to its use, possession, and enjoyment, you can take a deduction for the contribution in that later year.

Inventory. If you contribute inventory (property that you sell in the course of your business), the amount you can claim as a contribution deduction is the smaller of its fair market value on the day you contributed it or its basis. The basis of donated inventory is any cost incurred for the inventory in an earlier year that you would otherwise include in your opening inventory for the year of the contribution. You must remove the amount of your contribution deduction from your opening inventory. It is not part of the cost of goods sold.

If the cost of donated inventory is not included in your opening inventory, the inventory's basis is zero and you cannot claim a charitable contribution deduction. Treat the inventory's cost as you would ordinarily treat it under your method of accounting. For example, include the purchase price of inventory bought and donated in the same year in the cost of goods sold for that year.

Determining Fair Market Value

This section discusses general guidelines for determining the fair market value of various types of donated property. Publication 561 contains a more complete discussion.

Fair market value is the price at which property would change hands between a willing buyer and a willing seller, neither having to buy or sell, and both having reasonable knowledge of all the relevant facts.

Used clothing. The fair market value of used clothing and other personal items is usually far less than the price you paid for them. There are no fixed formulas or methods for finding the value of items of clothing.

You should claim as the value the price that buyers of used items actually pay in used clothing stores, such as consignment or thrift shops.

Household goods. The fair market value of used household goods, such as furniture, appliances, and linens, is usually much lower than the price paid when new. These items may have little or no market value because they are in a worn condition, out of style, or no longer useful. For these reasons, formulas (such as using a percentage of the cost to buy a new replacement item) are not acceptable in determining value.

You should support your valuation with photographs, canceled checks, receipts from your purchase of the items, or other evidence. Magazine or newspaper articles and photographs that describe the items and statements by the recipients of the items are also useful. Do not include any of this evidence with your tax return.

If the property is valuable because it is old or unique, see the discussion under *Paintings, Antiques, and Other Objects of Art* in Publication 561.

Cars, boats, and aircraft. If you contribute a car, boat, or aircraft to a charitable organization, you must determine its fair market value.

Certain commercial firms and trade organizations publish guides, commonly called "blue books," containing complete dealer sale prices or dealer average prices for recent model years. The guides may be published monthly or seasonally, and for different regions of the country. These guides also provide estimates for adjusting for unusual equipment, unusual mileage, and physical condition. The prices are not "official" and these publications are not considered an appraisal of any specific donated property. But they do provide clues for making an appraisal and suggest relative prices for comparison with current sales and offerings in your area.

These publications are sometimes available from public libraries or from the loan officer at a bank, credit union, or finance company.

Except for inexpensive small boats, the valuation of boats should be based on an appraisal by a marine surveyor because the physical condition is critical to the value.

Example. You donate your car to a local high school for use by students studying automobile repair. Your credit union told you that the "blue book" value of the car is $1,600. However, your car needs extensive repairs and, after some checking, you find that you could sell it for $750. You can deduct $750, the true fair market value of the car, as a charitable contribution.

Large quantities. If you contribute a large number of the same item, fair market value is the price at which comparable numbers of the item are being sold.

Example. You purchase 500 bibles for $1,000. The person who sells them to you says the retail value of these bibles is $3,000. If you contribute the bibles to a qualified organization, you can claim a deduction only for the price at which similar numbers of the same bible are currently being sold. Your charitable contribution is $1,000, unless you can show that similar numbers of that bible were selling at a different price at the time of the contribution.

Giving Property that Has Decreased in Value

If you contribute property with a fair market value that is less than your basis in it, your deduction is limited to its fair market value. You cannot claim a deduction for the difference between the property's basis and its fair market value.

Your **basis** in property is generally what you paid for it. If you need more information about basis, get Publication 551, *Basis of Assets.* You may want to get Publication 551 if you contribute property that you:

- Received as a gift or inheritance,
- Used in a trade, business, or activity conducted for profit, or
- Claimed a casualty loss deduction for.

Common examples of property that decreases in value include clothing, furniture, appliances, and cars.

Giving Property that Has Increased in Value

If you contribute property with a fair market value that is more than your basis in it, you may have to **reduce the fair market value** by the amount of appreciation (increase in value) when you figure your deduction.

Your basis in property is generally what you paid for it. If you need more information about basis, get Publication 551.

Different rules apply to figuring your deduction, depending on whether the property is:

1. Ordinary income property, or
2. Capital gain property.

Ordinary Income Property

Property is ordinary income property if its sale at fair market value on the date it was contributed would have resulted in ordinary income or in short-term capital gain. Examples of ordinary income property are inventory, works of art created by the donor, manuscripts prepared by the donor, and capital assets (defined later, under *Capital Gain Property*) held 1 year or less.

Property used in a trade or business. Property used in a trade or business is considered ordinary income property to the extent of any gain that would have been treated as ordinary income because of depreciation had the property been sold at its fair market value at the time of contribution. See chapter 3 of Publication 544, *Sales and Other Dispositions of Assets,* for the kinds of property to which this rule applies.

Amount of deduction. The amount you can deduct for a contribution of ordinary income property is its fair market value *less* the amount that would be ordinary income or short-term capital gain if you sold the property for its fair market value. Generally, this rule limits the deduction to your basis in the property.

Example. You donate stock that you held for 5 months to your church. The fair market value of the stock on the day you donate it is $1,000, but you paid only $800 (your basis). Because the $200 of appreciation would be short-term capital gain if you sold the stock, your deduction is limited to $800 (fair market value less the appreciation).

Exception. Do not reduce your charitable contribution if you include the ordinary or capital gain income in your gross income in the same year as the contribution. See *Ordinary or capital gain income included in gross income* under *Capital Gain Property,* next, if you need more information.

Capital Gain Property

Property is capital gain property if its sale at fair market value on the date of the contribution would have resulted in long-term capital gain. Capital gain property includes capital assets held more than 1 year.

Capital assets. Capital assets include most items of property that you own and use for personal purposes or investment. Examples of capital assets are stocks, bonds, jewelry, coin or stamp collections, and cars or furniture used for personal purposes.

For purposes of figuring your charitable contribution, capital assets also include certain real property and depreciable property used in your trade or business and, generally, held more than 1 year. (You may have to treat this property as partly ordinary income property and partly capital gain property.)

Real property. Real property is land and generally anything that is built on, growing on, or attached to land.

Depreciable property. Depreciable property is property used in business or held for the production of income and for which a depreciation deduction is allowed.

For more information about what is a capital asset, see chapter 2 of Publication 544.

Amount of deduction—general rule. When figuring your deduction for a gift of capital gain property, you usually can use the *fair market value* of the gift.

Exceptions. However, in certain situations, you must **reduce the fair market value** by any amount that would have been long-term capital gain if you had sold the property for its fair market value. Generally, this means reducing the fair market value to the property's cost or other basis. You must do this *if*:

1. The property (other than qualified appreciated stock) is contributed to certain private nonoperating foundations,
2. The contributed property is tangible personal property that is put to an unrelated use by the charity, or
3. You choose the 50% limit instead of the 30% limit, discussed later.

Contributions to private nonoperating foundations. The reduced deduction applies to contributions to all private nonoperating foundations other than those qualifying for the 50% limit, discussed later.

However, the reduced deduction does not apply to contributions of qualified appreciated stock. Qualified appreciated stock is any stock in a corporation that is capital gain property and for which market quotations are readily available on an established securities market on the day of the contribution. But stock in a corporation does not count as qualified appreciated stock to the extent you and your family contributed more than 10% of the value of all the outstanding stock in the corporation.

Contributions of tangible personal property. The term tangible personal property means any property, other than land or buildings, that can be seen or touched. It includes furniture, books, jewelry, paintings, and cars. The term **unrelated use** means a use that is unrelated to the exempt purpose or function of the charitable organization. For a governmental unit, it means the use of the contributed property for other than exclusively public purposes.

Example. If a painting contributed to an educational institution is used by that organization for educational purposes by being placed in its library for display and study by art students, the use is not an unrelated use. But if the painting is sold and the proceeds are used by the organization for educational purposes, the use is an unrelated use.

Ordinary or capital gain income included in gross income. You do not reduce your charitable contribution if you include the ordinary or capital gain income in your gross income in the same year as the contribution. This may happen when you transfer installment or discount obligations or when you assign income to a charitable organization. If you contribute an obligation received in a sale of property that is reported under the installment method, see Publication 537, *Installment Sales.*

Example. You donate an installment note to a qualified organization. The note has a fair market value of $10,000 and a basis to you of $7,000. As a result of the donation, you have a short-term capital gain of $3,000 ($10,000 − $7,000), which you include in your income for the year. Your charitable contribution is $10,000.

Bargain Sales

A bargain sale of property to a qualified organization (a sale or exchange for less than the property's fair market value) is partly a charitable contribution and partly a sale or exchange.

Part that is a sale or exchange. The part of the bargain sale that is a sale or exchange may result in a taxable gain. For more information on determining the amount of any taxable gain, see *Bargain sales to charity* in chapter 1 of Publication 544.

Part that is a charitable contribution. Figure the amount of your charitable contribution in three steps.

Step 1. Subtract the amount you received for the property from the property's fair market value at the time of sale. This gives you the fair market value of the contributed part.

Step 2. Find the adjusted basis of the contributed part. It equals:

$$\text{Adjusted basis} \atop \text{of entire property} \quad \times \quad \frac{\text{Fair market value of contributed part}}{\text{Fair market value of entire property}}$$

Step 3. Determine whether the amount of your charitable contribution is the fair market value of the contributed part (which you found in Step 1) or the adjusted basis of the contributed part (which you found in Step 2). Generally, if the property sold was capital gain property, your charitable contribution is the fair market value of the contributed part. If it was ordinary income property, your charitable contribution is the adjusted basis of the contributed part. See the ordinary income property and capital gain property rules (discussed earlier) for more information.

Example. You sell ordinary income property with a fair market value of $10,000 to a church for $2,000. Your basis is $4,000 and your adjusted gross income is $20,000. You make no other contributions during the year. The fair market value of the contributed part of the property is $8,000 ($10,000 − $2,000). The adjusted basis of the contributed part is $3,200 ($4,000 × [$8,000 ÷ $10,000]). Because the property is ordinary income property, your charitable contribution deduction is limited to the adjusted basis of the contributed part. You can deduct $3,200.

Penalty

You may be liable for a penalty if you overstate the value or adjusted basis of donated property.

20% penalty. The penalty is 20% of the amount by which you underpaid your tax because of the overstatement, if:

1. The value or adjusted basis claimed on your return is 200% or more of the correct amount, and
2. You underpaid your tax by more than $5,000 because of the overstatement.

40% penalty. The penalty is 40%, rather than 20%, if:

1. The value or adjusted basis claimed on your return is 400% or more of the correct amount, and

2. You underpaid your tax by more than $5,000 because of the overstatement.

When to Deduct

You can deduct your contributions only in the year you actually make them in cash or other property (or in a succeeding carryover year, as explained under *How To Figure Your Deduction When Limits Apply,* later). This applies whether you use the cash or an accrual method of accounting.

Time of making contribution. Usually, you make a contribution at the time of its unconditional delivery.

Checks. A check that you mail to a charity is considered delivered on the date you mail it.

Credit card. Contributions charged on your bank credit card are deductible in the year you make the charge.

Pay-by-phone account. If you use a pay-by-phone account, the date you make a contribution is the date the financial institution pays the amount. This date should be shown on the statement the financial institution sends to you.

Stock certificate. The gift to a charity of a properly endorsed stock certificate is completed on the date of mailing or other delivery to the charity or to the charity's agent. However, if you give a stock certificate to your agent or to the issuing corporation for transfer to the name of the charity, your gift is not completed until the date the stock is transferred on the books of the corporation.

Promissory note. If you issue and deliver a promissory note to a charitable organization as a contribution, it is not a contribution until you make the note payments.

Option. If you grant an option to buy real property at a bargain price to a charitable organization, you cannot take a deduction until the organization exercises the option.

Borrowed funds. If you make a contribution with borrowed funds, you can deduct the contribution in the year you make it, regardless of when you repay the loan.

Conditional gift. If your contribution is a conditional gift that depends on a future act or event that may not take place, you cannot take a deduction. But if there is only a negligible chance that the act or event will not take place, you can take a deduction.

If your contribution would be undone by a later act or event, you cannot take a deduction. But if there is only a negligible chance the act or event will take place, you can take a deduction.

Example 1. You donate cash to a local school board, which is a political subdivision of a state, to help build a school gym. The school board will refund the money to you if it does not collect enough to build the gym. You cannot deduct your gift as a charitable contribution until there is no chance of a refund.

Example 2. You donate land to a city for as long as the city uses it for a public park. The city does plan to use the land for a park, and there is no chance (or only a negligible chance) of the land being used for any different purpose. You can deduct your charitable contribution.

Limits on Deductions

If your total contributions for the year are 20% or less of your adjusted gross income, you do not need to read this section. The limits discussed here do not apply to you.

The amount of your deduction may be limited to either **20%, 30%, or 50%** of your adjusted gross income, depending on the type of property you give and the type of organization you give it to. These limits are described below.

If your contributions are more than any of the limits that apply, see *Carryovers* under *How To Figure Your Deduction When Limits Apply*, later.

Out-of-pocket expenses. Amounts you spend performing services for a charitable organization, which qualify as charitable contributions, are subject to the limit of the organization. For example, the 50% limit applies to amounts you spend on behalf of a church, a 50% limit organization. These amounts are considered a contribution to a qualified organization.

50% Limit

The 50% limit applies to the total of all charitable contributions you make during the year. This means that your deduction for charitable contributions cannot be more than 50% of your adjusted gross income for the year.

Only limit for 50% organizations. The 50% limit is the only limit that applies to gifts to organizations listed below under *50% Limit Organizations.* But there is one exception.

Exception. The 30% limit also applies to these gifts if they are gifts of capital gain property for which you figure your deduction using fair market value without reduction for appreciation. (See *30% Limit* later.)

50% Limit Organizations

You can ask any organization whether it is a 50% limit organization, and most will be able to tell you. Or you may check IRS Publication 78 (described earlier).

Only the following types of organizations are 50% limit organizations.

1. Churches, and conventions or associations of churches.

2. Educational organizations with a regular faculty and curriculum that normally have a regularly enrolled student body attending classes on site.

3. Hospitals and certain medical research organizations associated with these hospitals.

4. Organizations that are operated only to receive, hold, invest, and administer property and to make expenditures to or for the benefit of state and municipal colleges and universities and that normally receive substantial support from the United States or any state or their political subdivisions, or from the general public.

5. The United States or any state, the District of Columbia, a U.S. possession (including Puerto Rico), a political subdivision of a state or U.S. possession, or an Indian tribal government or any of its subdivisions that perform substantial government functions.

6. Corporations, trusts, or community chests, funds, or foundations organized and operated only for charitable, religious, educational, scientific, or literary purposes, or to prevent cruelty to children or animals, or to foster certain national or international amateur sports competition. These organizations must be "publicly supported," which means they

normally must receive a substantial part of their support, other than income from their exempt activities, from direct or indirect contributions from the general public or from governmental units.

7. Organizations that may not qualify as "publicly supported" under (6) but that meet other tests showing they respond to the needs of the general public, not a limited number of donors or other persons. They must normally receive more than one-third of their support either from organizations described in (1) through (6), or from persons other than "disqualified persons."

8. Most organizations operated or controlled by, and operated for the benefit of, those organizations described in (1) through (7).

9. Private operating foundations.

10. Private nonoperating foundations that make qualifying distributions of 100% of contributions within 2 1/2 months following the year they receive the contribution. A deduction for charitable contributions to any of these private nonoperating foundations must be supported by evidence from the foundation confirming that it made the qualifying distributions timely. Attach a copy of this supporting data to your tax return.

11. A private foundation whose contributions are pooled into a common fund, if the foundation would be described in (8) above but for the right of substantial contributors to name the public charities that receive contributions from the fund. The foundation must distribute the common fund's income within 2 1/2 months following the tax year in which it was realized and must distribute the corpus not later than 1 year after the donor's death (or after the death of the donor's surviving spouse if the spouse can name the recipients of the corpus).

30% Limit

The 30% limit applies to the following gifts.

- Gifts of capital gain property to 50% limit organizations. (For other gifts of capital gain property, see *20% Limit,* next.) However, the 30% limit does not apply when you choose to reduce the fair market value of the property by the amount that would have been long-term capital gain if you had sold the property. Instead, only the 50% limit applies. See *Capital Gain Property,* earlier, and *Capital gain property election* under *How To Figure Your Deduction When Limits Apply,* later.

- Gifts (other than gifts of capital gain property—see *20% Limit,* next) **for the use** of any organization.

- Gifts (other than gifts of capital gain property—see *20% Limit,* next) to all qualified organizations other than 50% limit organizations. This includes gifts to veterans' organizations, fraternal societies, nonprofit cemeteries, and certain private nonoperating foundations.

Student living with you. Amounts you spend on behalf of a student living with you are subject to the 30% limit. These amounts are considered a contribution *for the use of* a qualified organization.

20% Limit

The 20% limit applies to all gifts of capital gain property to or for the use of qualified organizations (other than gifts of capital gain property to 50% limit organizations).

How to Figure Your Deduction When Limits Apply

If your contributions are subject to more than one of the limits just discussed, you can deduct them as follows.

1. Contributions subject only to the **50% limit,** up to 50% of your adjusted gross income.

2. Contributions subject to the **30% limit,** up to the **lesser** of:

   a. 30% of adjusted gross income, or

   b. 50% of adjusted gross income **minus** your contributions to 50% limit organizations, **including** contributions of capital gain property subject to the 30% limit.

3. Contributions of **capital gain property** subject to the **30% limit,** up to the **lesser** of:

   a. 30% of adjusted gross income, or

   b. 50% of adjusted gross income **minus** your other contributions to 50% limit organizations.

4. Contributions subject to the **20% limit,** up to the **lesser** of:

   a. 20% of adjusted gross income,

   b. 30% of adjusted gross income **minus** your contributions subject to the 30% limit,

   c. 30% of adjusted gross income **minus** your contributions of capital gain property subject to the 30% limit, or

   d. 50% of adjusted gross income **minus** the total of your contributions to 50% limit organizations and your contributions subject to the 30% limit.

If more than one of the limits described above limit your deduction for chari-table contributions, you may want to use the worksheet in Table E.3 to figure your deduction and your carryover.

Example. Your adjusted gross income is $50,000. During the year, you gave your church $2,000 cash and land with a fair market value of $28,000 and a basis of $22,000. You held the land for investment purposes. You do not choose to reduce the fair market value of the land by the appreciation in value. You also gave $5,000 cash to a private foundation to which the 30% limit applies.

The $2,000 cash donated to the church is considered first and is fully deductible. Your contribution to the private foundation is considered next. Because your contributions to 50% limit organizations ($2,000 + $28,000) are more than $25,000 (50% of $50,000), your contribution to the private foundation is not deductible for the year. It can be carried over to later years. See *Carryovers*, later. The gift of land is considered next. Your deduction for the land is limited to $15,000 (30% × $50,000). The unused part of the gift of land ($13,000) can be carried over. For this year, your deduction is limited to $17,000 ($2,000 + $15,000).

A *Filled-In Worksheet for Limit on Deductions* in Table E.4 shows this com-putation in detail.

Capital gain property election. You may choose the 50% limit for gifts of capital gain property to 50% limit organizations instead of the 30% limit that would otherwise apply. If you make this choice, you must reduce the fair market value of the property contributed by the appreciation in value that would have been long-term capital gain if the property had been sold.

This choice applies to all capital gain property contributed to 50% limit organizations during a tax year. It also applies to carryovers of this kind of contribution from an earlier tax year. For details, see *Carryover of capital gain property*, later.

You must make the choice on your original return or on an amended return filed by the due date for filing the original return.

Example. In the previous example, if you choose to have the 50% limit apply to the land (the 30% capital gain property) given to your church, you must reduce the fair market value of the property by the appreciation in value. Therefore, the amount of your charitable contribution for the land would be its basis to you of $22,000. You add this amount to the

Table E.3 *Worksheet for Limit on Deductions*

Who can use this worksheet. You can use this worksheet if you made charitable contributions during the year, and one or more of the limits described in this publication under *Limits on Deductions* apply to you. You cannot use this worksheet if you have a carryover of a charitable contribution from an earlier year.

General instructions:

- The terms used in this worksheet are explained earlier in this publication.
- If your answer to any line is less than zero, enter zero.
- For contributions of property, enter the property's fair market value unless you elected (or were required) to reduce the fair market value as explained under *Giving Property That Has Increased in Value*. In that case, enter the reduced amount.

Step 1. List your charitable contributions made during the year.

1. Enter your contributions to 50% limit organizations. (Include contributions of capital gain property if you reduced the property's fair market value. Do not include contributions of capital gain property deducted at fair market value.)	1
2. Enter your contributions to 50% limit organizations of capital gain property deducted at fair market value	2
3. Enter your contributions (other than of capital gain property) to qualified organizations that are not 50% limit organizations	3
4. Enter your contributions "for the use of" any qualified organization. (But do not enter here any amount that must be entered on line 6.)	4
5. Add lines 3 and 4	5
6. Enter your contributions of capital gain property to or for the use of any qualified organization. (But do not enter here any amount entered on line 1 or 2.)	6

Step 2. Figure your deduction for the year and your carryover to the next year.

7. Enter your adjusted gross income	7
8. Multiply line 7 by 0.5. This is your 50% limit	8

		Deduct this year	Carryover to next year
Contributions to 50% limit organizations			
9. Enter the smaller of line 1 or line 8	9		
10. Subtract line 9 from line 1	10		
11. Subtract line 9 from line 8	11		
Contributions not to 50% limit organizations			
12. Add lines 1 and 2	12		
13. Multiply line 7 by 0.3. This is your 30% limit	13		
14. Subtract line 12 from line 8	14		
15. Enter the smallest of line 5, 13, or 14	15		
16. Subtract line 15 from line 5	16		
17. Subtract line 15 from line 13	17		
Contributions of capital gain property to 50% limit organizations			
18. Enter the smallest of line 2, 11, or 13	18		
19. Subtract line 18 from line 2	19		
20. Subtract line 15 from line 14	20		
21. Subtract line 18 from line 13	21		
Contributions of capital gain property not to 50% limit organizations			
22. Multiply line 7 by 0.2. This is your 20% limit	22		
23. Enter the smallest of line 6, 17, 20, 21, or 22	23		
24. Subtract line 23 from line 6	24		

Step 3. Summarize your deductions and carryovers.

25. Add lines 9, 15, 18, and 23. Enter the total here and on Schedule A (Form 1040)	25	
26. Add lines 10, 16, 19, and 24. Enter the total here. Carry it forward to Schedule A next year	26	

Table E.4 *Filled-In Worksheet for Limit on Deductions*

Who can use this worksheet. You can use this worksheet if you made charitable contributions during the year, and one or more of the limits described in this publication under *Limits on Deductions* apply to you. You cannot use this worksheet if you have a carryover of a charitable contribution from an earlier year.

General instructions:
- The terms used in this worksheet are explained earlier in this publication.
- If your answer to any line is less than zero, enter zero.
- For contributions of property, enter the property's fair market value unless you elected (or were required) to reduce the fair market value as explained under *Giving Property That Has Increased in Value.* In that case, enter the reduced amount.

Step 1. List your charitable contributions made during the year.

1.	Enter your contributions to 50% limit organizations. (Include contributions of capital gain property if you reduced the property's fair market value. Do not include contributions of capital gain property deducted at fair market value.)	1 — 2,000
2.	Enter your contributions to 50% limit organizations of capital gain property deducted at fair market value	2 — 28,000
3.	Enter your contributions (other than of capital gain property) to qualified organizations that are not 50% limit organizations	3 — 5,000
4.	Enter your contributions "for the use of" any qualified organization. (But do not enter here any amount that must be entered on line 6.)	4 — -0-
5.	Add lines 3 and 4.	5 — 5,000
6.	Enter your contributions of capital gain property to or for the use of any qualified organization. (But do not enter here any amount entered on line 1 or 2.)	6 — -0-

Step 2. Figure your deduction for the year and your carryover to the next year.

		Deduct this year	Carryover to next year
7. Enter your adjusted gross income	7 — 50,000		
8. Multiply line 7 by 0.5. This is your 50% limit	8 — 25,000		
Contributions to 50% limit organizations			
9. Enter the smaller of line 1 or line 8.	9	2,000	
10. Subtract line 9 from line 1.	10		-0-
11. Subtract line 9 from line 8.	11 — 23,000		
Contributions not to 50% limit organizations			
12. Add lines 1 and 2.	12 — 30,000		
13. Multiply line 7 by 0.3. This is your 30% limit.	13 — 15,000		
14. Subtract line 12 from line 8.	14 — -0-		
15. Enter the smallest of line 5, 13, or 14.	15	-0-	
16. Subtract line 15 from line 5.	16		5,000
17. Subtract line 15 from line 13.	17 — 15,000		
Contributions of capital gain property to 50% limit organizations			
18. Enter the smallest of line 2, 11, or 13.	18	15,000	
19. Subtract line 18 from line 2.	19		13,000
20. Subtract line 15 from line 14.	20 — -0-		
21. Subtract line 18 from line 13.	21 — -0-		
Contributions of capital gain property not to 50% limit organizations			
22. Multiply line 7 by 0.2. This is your 20% limit.	22 — 10,000		
23. Enter the smallest of line 6, 17, 20, 21, or 22	23	-0-	
24. Subtract line 23 from line 6.	24		-0-

Step 3. Summarize your deductions and carryovers.

25.	Add lines 9, 15, 18, and 23. Enter the total here and on Schedule A (Form 1040).	25	17,000
26.	Add lines 10, 16, 19, and 24. Enter the total here. Carry it forward to Schedule A next year.	26	18,000

$2,000 cash contributed to the church. You can now deduct $1,000 of the amount donated to the private foundation because your contributions to 50% limit organizations ($2,000 + $22,000) are $1,000 less than the 50%-of-adjusted-gross-income limit. Your total deduction for the year is $25,000 ($2,000 cash to your church, $22,000 for property donated to your church, and $1,000 cash to the private foundation). You can carry over to later years the part of your contribution to the private foundation that you could not deduct ($4,000).

Carryovers

You can carry over your contributions that you are not able to deduct in the current year because they exceed your adjusted-gross-income limits. You can deduct the excess in each of the next 5 years until it is used up, but not beyond that time. Your total contributions deduction for the year to which you carry your contributions cannot exceed 50% of your adjusted gross income for that year.

Contributions you carry over are subject to the same percentage limits in the year to which they are carried. For example, contributions subject to the 20% limit in the year in which they are made are 20% limit contributions in the year to which they are carried.

For each category of contributions, you deduct carryover contributions only after deducting all allowable contributions in that category for the current year. If you have carryovers from 2 or more prior years, use the carryover from the earlier year first.

Example 1. Last year, you contributed $11,000 to a 50% limit organization, but because of the limit you deducted only $10,000 and carried over $1,000 to this year. This year your adjusted gross income is $20,000 and you contribute $9,500 to a 50% limit organization. You can deduct $10,000 (50% of $20,000) this year. Consequently, in addition to your contribution of $9,500 for this year, you can deduct $500 of your carryover contribution from last year. You can carry over the $500 balance of your carryover from last year to next year.

Example 2. This year your adjusted gross income is $24,000. You make cash contributions of $6,000 to which the 50% limit applies and $3,000 to which the 30% limit applies. You have a contribution carryover from last year of $5,000 for capital gain property contributed to a 50% limit organization and subject to the 30% limit for contributions of capital gain property.

Your contribution deduction for this year is limited to $12,000 (50% of $24,000). Your 50% limit contributions of $6,000 are fully deductible.

The deduction for your 30% limit contributions of $3,000 is limited to $1,000. This is the lesser of:

1. $7,200 (30% of $24,000), or
2. $1,000 ($12,000 minus $11,000).

(The $12,000 amount is 50% of $24,000, your adjusted gross income. The $11,000 amount is the sum of your current and carryover contributions to 50% limit organizations, $6,000 + $5,000.)

The deduction for your $5,000 carryover is subject to the 30% limit for contributions of capital gain property. This means it is limited to the smaller of:

1. $7,200 (your 30% limit), or
2. $6,000 ($12,000, your 50% limit, minus $6,000, the amount of your cash contributions to 50% limit organizations this year).

Since your $5,000 carryover is less than both $7,200 and $6,000, you can deduct it in full.

Your deduction is $12,000 ($6,000 + $1,000 + $5,000). You carry over the $2,000 balance of your 30% limit contributions for this year to next year.

Carryover of capital gain property. If you carry over contributions of capital gain property subject to the 30% limit and you choose in the next year to use the 50% limit and take appreciation into account, you must refigure the carryover. You reduce the fair market value of the property by the appreciation and reduce that result by the amount actually deducted in the previous year.

   Example. Last year your adjusted gross income was $50,000 and you contributed capital gain property valued at $27,000 to a 50% limit organization and did not choose to use the 50% limit. Your basis in the property was $20,000. Your deduction was limited to $15,000 (30% of $50,000), and you carried over $12,000. This year your adjusted gross income is $60,000 and you contribute capital gain property valued at $25,000 to a 50% limit organization. Your basis in the property is $24,000 and you choose to use the 50% limit. You must refigure your carryover as if you had taken appreciation into account last year as well as this year. Because the amount of your contribution last year would have been $20,000 (the property's basis) instead of the $15,000 you actually deducted, your refigured carryover is $5,000 ($20,000 − $15,000). Your total deduction this year is $29,000 (your $24,000 current contribution plus your $5,000 carryover).

Additional rules for carryovers. Special rules exist for computing carryovers if you:

- Were married in some years but not others,
- Had different spouses in different years,
- Change from a separate return to a joint return in a later year,
- Change from a joint return to a separate return in a later year,
- Had a net operating loss,
- Claim the standard deduction in a carryover year, or
- Become a widow or widower.

Because of their complexity and the limited number of taxpayers to whom these additional rules apply, they are not discussed in this publication. If you need to compute a carryover and you are in one of these situations, you may want to consult with a tax practitioner.

Records to Keep

You must keep records to prove the amount of the cash and noncash contributions you make during the year. The kind of records you must keep depends on the amount of your contributions and whether they are cash or noncash contributions.

   Note. An organization generally must give you a written statement if it receives a payment from you that is more than $75 and is partly a contribution and partly for goods or services. (See *Contributions from which You Benefit* under *Contributions You Can Deduct*, earlier.) Keep the statement for your records. It may satisfy all or part of the recordkeeping requirements explained in the following discussions.

Cash Contributions

Cash contributions include those paid by cash, check, credit card, or payroll deduction. They also include your out-of-pocket expenses when donating your services.

For a contribution made in cash, the records you must keep depend on whether the contribution is:

1. Less than $250, or
2. $250 or more.

Amount of contribution. In figuring whether your contribution is $250 or more, do not combine separate contributions. For example, if you gave your church $25 each week, your weekly payments do not have to be combined. Each payment is a separate contribution.

If contributions are made by payroll deduction, the deduction from each paycheck is treated as a separate contribution.

If you made a payment that is partly for goods and services, as described earlier under *Contributions from which You Benefit*, your contribution is the amount of the payment that is more than the value of the goods and services.

Contributions of Less than $250

For each cash contribution that is less than $250, you must keep one of the following.

1. A canceled check, **or** a legible and readable account statement that shows:
   a. If payment was by check—the check number, amount, date posted, and to whom paid,
   b. If payment was by electronic funds transfer—the amount, date posted, and to whom paid, or
   c. If payment was charged to a credit card—the amount, transaction date, and to whom paid.
2. A receipt (or a letter or other written communication) from the charitable organization showing the name of the organization, the date of the contribution, and the amount of the contribution.
3. Other reliable written records that include the information described in 2. Records may be considered reliable if they were made at or near the time of the contribution, were regularly kept by you, or if, in the case of small donations, you have buttons, emblems, or other tokens, that are regularly given to persons making small cash contributions.

Car expenses. If you claim expenses directly related to use of your car in giving services to a qualified organization, you must keep reliable written records of your expenses. Whether your records are considered reliable depends on all the facts and circumstances. Generally, they may be considered reliable if you made them regularly and at or near the time you had the expenses.

Your records must show the name of the organization you were serving and the date each time you used your car for a charitable purpose. If you use the standard mileage rate, your records must show the miles you drove your car for the charitable purpose. If you deduct your actual expenses, your records must show the costs of operating the car that are directly related to a charitable purpose.

See *Car expenses* under *Out-of-Pocket Expenses in Giving Services*, earlier, for the expenses you can deduct.

Contributions of $250 or More

You can claim a deduction for a contribution of $250 or more only if you have an acknowledgement of your contribution from the qualified organization or certain payroll deduction records.

If you made more than one contribution of $250 or more, you must have either a separate acknowledgement for each or one acknowledgement that shows your total contributions.

Acknowledgement. The acknowledgement must meet these tests.
1. It must be written.
2. It must include:
   a. The amount of cash you contributed,
   b. Whether the qualified organization gave you any goods or services as a result of your contribution (other than certain token items and membership benefits), and
   c. A description and good faith estimate of the value of any goods or services described in b. If the only benefit you received was an intangible religious benefit (such as admission to a religious ceremony) that generally is not sold in a commercial transaction outside the donative context, the acknowledgement must say so and does not need to describe or estimate the value of the benefit.

3. You must get it on or before the earlier of:
   a. The date you file your return for the year you make the contribution, or
   b. The due date, including extensions, for filing the return.

Payroll deductions. If you make a contribution by payroll deduction, you do not need an acknowledgement from the qualified organization. But if your employer deducted $250 or more from a single paycheck, you must keep:

1. A pay stub, Form W-2, or other document furnished by your employer that proves the amount withheld, and

2. A pledge card or other document from the qualified organization that states the organization does not provide goods or services in return for any contribution made to it by payroll deduction.

Out-of-pocket expenses. If you render services to a qualified organization and have unreimbursed out-of-pocket expenses related to those services, you can satisfy the written acknowledgement requirement just discussed if:

1. You have adequate records to prove the amount of the expenses, and

2. By the required date, you get an acknowledgement from the qualified organization that contains:
   a. A description of the services you provided,
   b. A statement of whether or not the organization provided you any goods or services to reimburse you for the expenses you incurred,
   c. A description and a good faith estimate of the value of any goods or services (other than intangible religious benefits) provided to reimburse you, and
   d. A statement of any intangible religious benefits provided to you.

Noncash Contributions

For a contribution not made in cash, the records you must keep depend on whether your deduction for the contribution is:

1. Less than $250,
2. At least $250 but not more than $500,
3. Over $500 but not more than $5,000, or
4. Over $5,000.

Amount of contribution. In figuring whether your contribution is $250 or more, do not combine separate contributions. If you got goods or services in return, as described earlier in *Contributions from which You Benefit,* reduce your contribution by the value of those goods or services. If you figure your deduction by reducing the fair market value of the donated property by its appreciation, as described earlier in *Giving Property that Has Increased in Value*, your contribution is the reduced amount.

Deductions of Less than $250

If you make any noncash contribution, you must get and keep a receipt from the charitable organization showing:

1. The name of the charitable organization,
2. The date and location of the charitable contribution, and
3. A reasonably detailed description of the property.

A letter or other written communication from the charitable organization acknowledging receipt of the contribution and containing the information in 1, 2, and 3 will serve as a receipt.

You are not required to have a receipt where it is impractical to get one (for example, if you leave property at a charity's unattended drop site).

Additional records. You must also keep reliable written records for each item of donated property. Your written records must include the following information.

1. The name and address of the organization to which you contributed.
2. The date and location of the contribution.
3. A description of the property in detail reasonable under the circumstances. For a security, keep the name of the issuer, the type of security, and whether it is regularly traded on a stock exchange or in an over-the-counter market.
4. The fair market value of the property at the time of the contribution and how you figured the fair market value. If it was determined by appraisal, you should also keep a signed copy of the appraisal.
5. The cost or other basis of the property if you must reduce its fair market value by appreciation. Your records should also include the amount of the reduction and how you figured it. If you choose the 50% limit instead of the special 30% limit on certain capital gain property (discussed under *Capital gain property election*, earlier), you must keep a record showing the years for which you made the choice, contributions for the current year to which the choice applies, and carryovers from preceding years to which the choice applies.

6. The amount you claim as a deduction for the tax year as a result of the contribution, if you contribute less than your entire interest in the property during the tax year. Your records must include the amount you claimed as a deduction in any earlier years for contributions of other interests in this property. They must also include the name and address of each organization to which you contributed the other interests, the place where any such tangible property is located or kept, and the name of any person in possession of the property, other than the organization to which you contributed.

7. The terms of any conditions attached to the gift of property.

Deductions of at Least $250 But Not More than $500

If you claim a deduction of at least $250 but not more than $500 for a non-cash charitable contribution, you must get and keep an acknowledgement of your contribution from the qualified organization. If you made more than one contribution of $250 or more, you must have either a separate acknowledgement for each or one acknowledgement that shows your total contributions.

The acknowledgement must contain the information in items (1) through (3) listed under *Deductions of Less than $250*, earlier, and your written records must include the information listed in that discussion under *Additional records*.

The acknowledgement must also meet these tests.

1. It must be written.

2. It must include:

   a. A description (but not necessarily the value) of any property you contributed,

   b. Whether the qualified organization gave you any goods or services as a result of your contribution (other than certain token items and membership benefits), and

   c. A description and good faith estimate of the value of any goods or services described in b. If the only benefit you received was an intangible religious benefit (such as admission to a religious ceremony) that generally is not sold in a commercial transaction outside the donative context, the acknowledgement must say so and does not need to describe or estimate the value of the benefit.

3. You must get the acknowledgement on or before the earlier of:
   a. The date you file your return for the year you make the contribution, or
   b. The due date, including extensions, for filing the return.

Deductions Over $500 But Not Over $5,000

If you claim a deduction over $500 but not over $5,000 for a noncash chari- table contribution, you must have the acknowledgement and written records described under *Deductions of At Least $250 But Not More Than $500*. Your records must also include:

1. How you got the property, for example, by purchase, gift, bequest,' inheritance, or exchange.
2. The approximate date you got the property or, if created, produced, or manufactured by or for you, the approximate date the property was substantially completed.
3. The cost or other basis, and any adjustments to the basis, of property held less than 12 months and, if available, the cost or other basis of property held 12 months or more. This requirement, however, does not apply to publicly traded securities.

If you are not able to provide information on either the date you got the property or the cost basis of the property and you have a reasonable cause for not being able to provide this information, attach a statement of explana- tion to your return.

Deductions Over $5,000

If you claim a deduction of over $5,000 for a charitable contribution of one property item or a group of similar property items, you must have the acknowledgement and the written records described under *Deductions Over $500 But Not Over $5,000*. In figuring whether your deduction is over $5,000, combine your claimed deductions for all similar items donated to any charitable organization during the year.

Generally, you must also obtain a qualified written appraisal of the donated property from a qualified appraiser. See *Deductions of More Than $5,000* in Publication 561 for more information.

   Qualified conservation contribution. If the gift was a "qualified conserva- tion contribution," your records must also include the fair market value of the underlying property before and after the gift and the conservation purpose furthered by the gift. See *Qualified conservation contribution* in Publication 561 for more information.

How to Report

Report your charitable contributions on Schedule A of Form 1040.

If you made noncash contributions, you may also be required to fill out parts of Form 8283. See *Noncash contributions*, later.

Reporting expenses for student living with you. If you claim amounts paid for a student who lives with you, as described earlier under Expenses Paid for Student Living With You, you must submit with your return:

1. A copy of your agreement with the organization sponsoring the student placed in your household,
2. A summary of the various items you paid to maintain the student, and
3. A statement that gives:
   a. The date the student became a member of your household,
   b. The dates of his or her full-time attendance at school, and
   c. The name and location of the school.

Noncash contributions. If your *total* deduction for all noncash contributions for the year is **over $500,** you must complete Section A of **Form 8283,** and attach it to your Form 1040. However, do not complete Section A for items you must report on Section B. See *Deduction over $5,000 for one item*, next, for the items you must report on Section B.

The Internal Revenue Service can disallow your deduction for noncash charitable contributions if it is more than $500 and you do not submit a required Form 8283 with your return.

    Deduction over $5,000 for one item. You must complete Section B of Form 8283 for each item or group of items for which you claim a deduction of over $5,000. (However, if you contributed certain publicly traded securities, complete Section A instead.) In figuring whether your deduction is over $5,000, combine the claimed deductions for all similar items donated to any charitable organization during the year. The organization that received the property must complete and sign Part IV of Section B.

Form 8282. If an organization, within 2 years after the date of receipt of a contribution of property for which it was required to sign a Form 8283, sells, exchanges, or otherwise disposes of the property, the organization must file an information return with the Internal Revenue Service on Form 8282, *Donee Information Return,* and send you a copy of the form. However, if you have informed the organization that the appraised value of the donated item, or a specific item within a group of similar items, is $500 or less, the organization is not required to make a report on its sale of that item. For this purpose, all shares of nonpublicly traded stock or securities, or items that form a set, are considered to be one item.

How to Get Tax Help

You can get help with unresolved tax issues, order free publications and forms, ask tax questions, and get more information from the IRS in several ways. By selecting the method that is best for you, you will have quick and easy access to tax help.

Contacting Your Taxpayer Advocate. If you have attempted to deal with an IRS problem unsuccessfully, you should contact your Taxpayer Advocate.

The Taxpayer Advocate represents your interests and concerns within the IRS by protecting your rights and resolving problems that have not been fixed through normal channels. While Taxpayer Advocates cannot change the tax law or make a technical tax decision, they can clear up problems that resulted from previous contacts and ensure that your case is given a complete and impartial review.

To contact your Taxpayer Advocate:
• Call the Taxpayer Advocate at 1-877-777-4778.
• Call the IRS at 1-800-829-1040.
• Call, write, or fax the Taxpayer Advocate office in your area.
• Call 1-800-829-4059 if you are a TTY/TDD user.

For more information, see Publication 1546, *The Taxpayer Advocate Service of the IRS.*

Free tax services. To find out what services are available, get Publication 910, *Guide to Free Tax Services.* It contains a list of free tax publications and an index of tax topics. It also describes other free tax information services, including tax education and assistance programs and a list of TeleTax topics.

Personal computer. With your personal computer and modem, you can access the IRS on the Internet at www.irs.gov. While visiting our web site, you can select:

- *Frequently Asked Tax Questions* (located under *Taxpayer Help & Ed*) to find answers to questions you may have.

- *Forms & Pubs* to download forms and publications or search for forms and publications by topic or keyword.

- *Fill-in Forms* (located under *Forms & Pubs*) to enter information while the form is displayed and then print the completed form.

- *Tax Info For You* to view Internal Revenue Bulletins published in the last few years.

- *Tax Regs in English* to search regulations and the Internal Revenue Code (under *United States Code (USC)*).

- *Digital Dispatch* and *IRS Local News Net* (both located under *Tax Info For Business*) to receive our electronic newsletters on hot tax issues and news.

- *Small Business Corner* (located under *Tax Info For Business*) to get information on starting and operating a small business.

You can also reach us with your computer using File Transfer Protocol at **ftp.irs.gov.**

TaxFax Service. Using the phone attached to your fax machine, you can receive forms and instructions by calling 703-368-9694. Follow the directions from the prompts. When you order forms, enter the catalog number for the form you need. The items you request will be faxed to you.

Phone. Many services are available by phone.

- *Ordering forms, instructions, and publications.* Call **1-800-829-3676** to order current and prior year forms, instructions, and publications.

- *Asking tax questions.* Call the IRS with your tax questions at **1-800-829-1040.**

- *TTY/TDD equipment.* If you have access to TTY/TDD equipment, call **1-800-829-4059** to ask tax questions or to order forms and publications.

- *TeleTax topics.* Call **1-800-829-4477** to listen to pre-recorded messages covering various tax topics.

Evaluating the quality of our telephone services. To ensure that IRS representatives give accurate, courteous, and professional answers, we evaluate the quality of our telephone services in several ways.

- A second IRS representative sometimes monitors live telephone calls. That person only evaluates the IRS assistor and does not keep a record of any taxpayer's name or tax identification number.

- We sometimes record telephone calls to evaluate IRS assistors objectively. We hold these recordings no longer than one week and use them only to measure the quality of assistance.

- We value our customers' opinions. Throughout this year, we will be surveying our customers for their opinions on our service.

Walk-in. You can walk in to many post offices, libraries, and IRS offices to pick up certain forms, instructions, and publications. Also, some libraries and IRS offices have:

- An extensive collection of products available to print from a CD-ROM or photocopy from reproducible proofs.

- The Internal Revenue Code, regulations, Internal Revenue Bulletins, and Cumulative Bulletins available for research purposes.

Mail. You can send your order for forms, instructions, and publications to the Distribution Center nearest to you and receive a response within 10 workdays after your request is received. Find the address that applies to your part of the country.

- Western part of United States:
  Western Area Distribution Center
  Rancho Cordova, CA 95743-0001

- Central part of United States:
  Central Area Distribution Center
  P.O. Box 8903
  Bloomington, IL 61702-8903

- Eastern part of United States and foreign addresses:
  Eastern Area Distribution Center
  P.O. Box 85074
  Richmond, VA 23261-5074

CD-ROM. You can order IRS Publication 1796, *Federal Tax Products on CD-ROM,* and obtain:

- Current tax forms, instructions, and publications.

- Prior-year tax forms, instructions, and publications.

- Popular tax forms which may be filled in electronically, printed out for submission, and saved for recordkeeping.
- Internal Revenue Bulletins.

The CD-ROM can be purchased from National Technical Information Service (NTIS) by calling **1-877-233-6767** or on the Internet at **www.irs.gov/cdorders**. The first release is available in mid-December and the final release is available in late January.

IRS Publication 3207, *The Small Business Resource Guide*, is an interactive CD-ROM that contains information important to small businesses. It is available in mid-February. You can get one free copy by calling **1-800-829-3676.**

Appendix F

IRS Publication 561—Determining the Value of Donated Property (Rev. February 2000) Cat. No. 15109Q

Introduction

This publication is designed to help donors and appraisers determine the value of property (other than cash) that is given to qualified organizations. It also explains what kind of information you must have to support the charitable contribution deduction you claim on your return.

This publication does not discuss how to figure the amount of your deduction for charitable contributions or written records and substantiation required. See Publication 526, *Charitable Contributions*, for this information.

Useful Items

You may want to see:

Publication

- **526** Charitable Contributions
- **535** Business Expenses

Form (and Instructions)

- **8282** Donee Information Return
- **8283** Noncash Charitable Contributions

See *How to Get More Information,* near the end of this publication, for information about getting these publications and forms.

What Is Fair Market Value (FMV)?

To figure how much you may deduct for property that you contribute, you must first determine its fair market value on the date of the contribution.

Fair market value. Fair market value (FMV) is the price that property would sell for on the open market. It is the price that would be agreed on between a willing buyer and a willing seller, with neither being required to act, and both having reasonable knowledge of the relevant facts. If you put a restriction on the use of property you donate, the FMV must reflect that restriction.

Example 1. If you give used clothing to the Salvation Army, the FMV would be the price that typical buyers actually pay for clothing of this age, condition, style, and use. Usually, such items are worth far less than what you paid for them.

Example 2. If you donate land and restrict its use to agricultural purposes, you must value the land at its value for agricultural purposes, even though it would have a higher FMV if it were not restricted.

Factors. In making and supporting the valuation of property, all factors affecting value are relevant and must be considered. These include:

1. The cost or selling price of the item,
2. Sales of comparable properties,
3. Replacement cost, and
4. Opinions of experts.

These factors are discussed later. Also, see *Table F.1* for a summary of questions to ask as you consider each factor.

Date of contribution. Ordinarily, the date of a contribution is the date that the transfer of the property takes place.

Stock. If you deliver, without any conditions, a properly endorsed stock certificate to a qualified organization or to an agent of the organization, the date of the contribution is the date of delivery. If the certificate is mailed and received through the regular mail, it is the date of mailing. If you deliver the certificate to a bank or broker acting as your agent or to the issuing corporation or its agent, for transfer into the name of the organization, the date of the contribution is the date the stock is transferred on the books of the corporation.

Table F.1 *Determining FMV*	
When you use this factor:	**You should consider these questions:**
Cost or Selling Price	Was the purchase or sale of the property reasonably close to the date of contribution?
	Was any increase or decrease in value, as compared to your cost, at a reasonable rate?
	Do the terms of purchase or sale limit what can be done with the property?
	Was there an arm's length offer to buy the property close to the valuation date?
Sales of Comparable Properties	How similar is the property sold to the property donated?
	How close is the date of sale to the valuation date?
	Was the sale at arm's length?
	What was the condition of the market at the time of sale?
Replacement Cost	What would it cost to replace the donated property?
	Is there a reasonable relationship between replacement cost and FMV?
	Is the supply of the donated property more or less than the demand for it?
Opinions of Experts	Is the expert knowledgeable and competent?
	Is the opinion thorough and supported by facts and experience?

Options. If you grant an option to a qualified organization to purchase real property, you have not made a charitable contribution until the organization exercises the option. The amount of the contribution is the FMV of the property on the date the option is exercised minus the exercise price.

Example. You grant an option to a local university, which is a qualified organization, to purchase real property. Under the option, the university could purchase the property at any time during a 2-year period for $40,000. The FMV of the property on the date the option is granted is $50,000.

In the following tax year, the university exercises the option. The FMV of the property on the date the option is exercised is $55,000. Therefore, you have made a charitable contribution of $15,000 ($55,000, the FMV, minus $40,000, the exercise price) in the tax year the option is exercised.

Determining Fair Market Value

Determining the value of donated property would be a simple matter if you could rely only on fixed formulas, rules, or methods. Usually it is not that simple. Using such formulas, etc., seldom results in an acceptable determination of FMV. There is no single formula that always applies when determining the value of property.

This is not to say that a valuation is only guesswork. You must consider all the facts and circumstances connected with the property, such as its desirability, use, and scarcity.

For example, donated furniture should not be evaluated at some fixed rate such as 15% of the cost of new replacement furniture. When the furniture is contributed, it may be out of style or in poor condition, therefore having little or no market value. On the other hand, it may be an antique, the value of which could not be determined by using any formula.

Cost or Selling Price of the Donated Property

Your cost of the property or the actual selling price received by the qualified organization may be the best indication of its FMV. However, because conditions in the market change, the cost or selling price of property may have less weight if the property was not bought or sold reasonably close to the date of contribution.

The cost or selling price is a good indication of the property's value if:

1. The purchase or sale took place close to the valuation date in an open market,
2. The purchase or sale was at "arm's-length,"
3. The buyer and seller knew all relevant facts,
4. The buyer and seller did not have to act, and
5. The market did not change between the date of purchase or sale and the valuation date.

    Example. Tom Morgan, who is not a dealer in gems, bought an assortment of gems for $5,000 from a promoter. The promoter claimed that the price was "wholesale" even though he and other dealers made similar sales at similar prices to other persons who were not dealers. The promoter said that if Tom kept the gems for more than one year and then gave them to charity, Tom could claim a charitable deduction of $15,000, which, according to the promoter, would be the value of the gems at the time of contribution. Tom gave the gems to a qualified charity 13 months after buying them.

The selling price for these gems had not changed from the date of purchase to the date he donated them to charity. The best evidence of FMV depends on actual transactions and not on some artificial estimate. The $5,000 charged Tom and others is, therefore, the best evidence of the maximum FMV of the gems.

Terms of the purchase or sale. The terms of the purchase or sale should be considered in determining FMV if they influenced the price. These terms include any restrictions, understandings, or covenants limiting the use or disposition of the property.

Rate of increase or decrease in value. Unless you can show that there were unusual circumstances, it is assumed that the increase or decrease in the value of your donated property from your cost has been at a reasonable rate. For time adjustments, an appraiser may consider published price indexes for information on general price trends, building costs, commodity costs, securities, and works of art sold at auction in arm's-length sales.

    Example. Bill Brown bought a painting for $10,000. Thirteen months later he gave it to an art museum, claiming a charitable deduction of $15,000 on his tax return. The appraisal of the painting should include information showing that there were unusual circumstances that justify a 50% increase in value for the 13 months Bill held the property.

Arm's-length offer. An arm's-length offer to buy the property close to the valuation date may help to prove its value if the person making the offer was willing and able to complete the transaction. To rely on an offer, you should be able to show proof of the offer and the specific amount to be paid. Offers to buy property other than the donated item will help to determine value if the other property is reasonably similar to the donated property.

Sales of Comparable Properties

The sales prices of properties similar to the donated property are often important in determining the FMV. The weight to be given to each sale depends on the following:

1. The degree of similarity between the property sold and the donated property.

2. The time of the sale—whether it was close to the valuation date.

3. The circumstances of the sale—whether it was at arm's-length with a knowledgeable buyer and seller, with neither having to act.

4. The conditions of the market in which the sale was made—whether unusually inflated or deflated.

The comparable sales method of valuing real estate is explained later under *Valuation of Various Kinds of Property*.

Example 1. Mary Black, who is not a book dealer, paid a promoter $10,000 for 500 copies of a single edition of a modern translation of the Bible. The promoter had claimed that the price was considerably less than the "retail" price, and gave her a statement that the books had a total retail value of $30,000. The promoter advised her that if she kept the Bibles for more than one year and then gave them to a qualified organization, she could claim a charitable deduction for the "retail" price of $30,000. Thirteen months later she gave all the Bibles to a church that she selected from a list provided by the promoter. At the time of her donation, wholesale dealers were selling similar quantities of Bibles to the general public for $10,000.

The FMV of the Bibles is $10,000, the price at which similar quantities of Bibles were being sold to others at the time of the contribution.

Example 2. Assume the same facts as in Example 1, except that the promoter gave Mary Black a second option. The promoter said that if Mary wanted a charitable deduction within one year of the purchase, she could buy the 500 Bibles at the "retail" price of $30,000, paying only $10,000 in cash and giving a promissory note for the remaining $20,000. The principal and interest on the note would not be due for 12 years. According to the promoter, Mary could then, within one year of the purchase, give the Bibles to a qualified organization and claim the full $30,000 retail price as a charitable contribution. She purchased the Bibles under the second option and, 3 months later, gave them to a church, which will use the books for church purposes.

At the time of the gift, the promoter was selling similar lots of Bibles for either $10,000 or $30,000. The difference between the two prices was solely at the discretion of the buyer. The promoter was a willing seller for $10,000. Therefore, the value of Mary's contribution of the Bibles is $10,000, the amount at which similar lots of Bibles could be purchased from the promoter by members of the general public.

Replacement Cost

The cost of buying, building, or manufacturing property similar to the donated item should be considered in determining FMV. However, there must be a reasonable relationship between the replacement cost and the FMV.

The replacement cost is the amount it would cost to replace the donated item on the valuation date. Often there is no relationship between the replacement cost and the FMV. If the supply of the donated property is more or less than the demand for it, the replacement cost becomes less important.

To determine the replacement cost of the donated property, find the "estimated replacement cost new." Then subtract from this figure an amount for depreciation due to the physical condition and obsolescence of the donated property. You should be able to show the relationship between the depreciated replacement cost and the FMV, as well as how you arrived at the "estimated replacement cost new."

Opinions of Experts

Generally, the weight given to an expert's opinion on matters such as the authenticity of a coin or a work of art, or the most profitable and best use of a piece of real estate, depends on the knowledge and competence of the expert and the thoroughness with which the opinion is supported by experience and facts. For an expert's opinion to deserve much weight, the facts must support the opinion. For additional information, see *Appraisals*, later.

Problems in Determining Fair Market Value

There are a number of problems in determining the FMV of donated property.

Unusual Market Conditions

The sale price of the property itself in an arm's-length transaction in an open market is often the best evidence of its value. When you rely on sales of comparable property, the sales must have been made in an open market. If those sales were made in a market that was artificially supported or stimulated so as not to be truly representative, the prices at which the sales were made will not indicate the FMV.

For example, liquidation sale prices usually do not indicate the FMV. Also, sales of stock under unusual circumstances, such as sales of small lots, forced sales, and sales in a restricted market, may not represent the FMV.

Selection of Comparable Sales

Using sales of comparable property is an important method for determining the FMV of donated property. However, the amount of weight given to a sale depends on the degree of similarity between the comparable and the donated properties. The degree of similarity must be close enough so that this selling price would have been given consideration by reasonably well-informed buyers or sellers of the property.

   Example. You give a rare, old book to your former college. The book is a third edition and is in poor condition because of a missing back cover. You discover that there was a sale for $300, near the valuation date, of a first edition of the book that was in good condition. Although the contents are the same, the books are not at all similar because of the different editions and their physical condition. Little consideration would be given to the selling price of the $300 property by knowledgeable buyers or sellers.

Future Events

You may not consider unexpected events happening after your donation of property in making the valuation. You may consider only the facts known at the time of the gift, and those that could be reasonably expected at the time of the gift.

Example. You give farmland to a qualified charity. The transfer provides that your mother will have the right to all income and full use of the property for her life. Even though your mother dies one week after the transfer, the value of the property on the date it is given is its present value, subject to the life interest as estimated from actuarial tables. You may not take a higher deduction because the charity received full use and possession of the land only one week after the transfer.

Using Past Events to Predict the Future

A common error is to rely too much on past events that do not fairly reflect the probable future earnings and FMV.

Example. You give all your rights in a successful patent to your favorite charity. Your records show that before the valuation date there were three stages in the patent's history of earnings. First, there was rapid growth in earnings when the invention was introduced. Then, there was a period of high earnings when the invention was being exploited. Finally, there was a decline in earnings when competing inventions were introduced. The entire history of earnings may be relevant in estimating the future earnings. However, the appraiser must not rely too much on the stage of rapid growth in earnings, or of high earnings. The market conditions at those times do not represent the condition of the market at the valuation date. What is most significant is the trend of decline in earnings up to the valuation date.

Valuation of Various Kinds of Property

This section contains information on determining the FMV of ordinary kinds of donated property. For information on appraisals, see *Appraisals*, later.

Household Goods

The FMV of used household goods, such as furniture, appliances, and linens, is usually much lower than the price paid when new. Such used property may have little or no market value because of its worn condition. It may be out of style or no longer useful.

If the property is valuable because it is old or unique, see the discussion under *Paintings, Antiques, and Other Objects of Art.*

Used Clothing

Used clothing and other personal items are usually worth far less than the price you paid for them. Valuation of items of clothing does not lend itself to fixed formulas or methods.

The price that buyers of used items actually pay in used clothing stores, such as consignment or thrift shops, is an indication of the value.

For valuable furs or very expensive gowns, an appraisal summary may have to be sent with your tax return.

Jewelry and Gems

Jewelry and gems are of such a specialized nature that it is almost always necessary to get an appraisal by a specialized jewelry appraiser. The appraisal should describe, among other things, the style of the jewelry, the cut and setting of the gem, and whether it is now in fashion. If not in fashion, the possibility of having the property redesigned, recut, or reset should be reported in the appraisal. The stone's coloring, weight, cut, brilliance, and flaws should be reported and analyzed. Sentimental personal value has no effect on FMV. But if the jewelry was owned by a famous person, its value might increase.

Paintings, Antiques, and Other Objects of Art

Your deduction for contributions of paintings, antiques, and other objects of art, should be supported by a written appraisal from a qualified and reputable source, unless the deduction is $5,000 or less. Examples of information that should be included in appraisals of art objects—paintings in particular—are found later under *Qualified Appraisal.*

Art valued at $20,000 or more. If you claim a deduction of $20,000 or more for donations of art, you must attach a complete copy of the signed appraisal to your return. For individual objects valued at $20,000 or more, a photograph of a size and quality fully showing the object, preferably an 8 × 10 inch color photograph or a color transparency no smaller than 4 × 5 inches, must be provided upon request.

Art valued at $50,000 or more. If you donate an item of art that has been appraised at $50,000 or more, you can request a **Statement of Value** for that item from the IRS. You must request the statement before filing the tax return that reports the donation. Your request must include the following:

1. A copy of a qualified appraisal of the item (see *Qualified Appraisal*, later).

2. A $2,500 check or money order payable to the Internal Revenue Service for the user fee that applies to your request regarding one, two, or three items of art (add $250 for each item in excess of three).

3. A completed appraisal summary (Section B of Form 8283, *Noncash Charitable Contributions*).

4. The location of the IRS District Office that has examination responsibility for your area.

If your request lacks essential information, you will be notified and given 30 days to provide the missing information.

Refunds. You can withdraw your request for a Statement of Value at any time before it is issued. However, the IRS will not refund the user fee if you do.

If the IRS declines to issue a Statement of Value in the interest of efficient tax administration, the IRS will refund the user fee.

Authenticity. The authenticity of the donated art must be determined by the appraiser. Certificates of authenticity may be useful, but this depends on the genuineness of the certificate and the qualifications of the authenticator.

Physical condition. Important items in the valuation of antiques and art are physical condition and extent of restoration. These have a significant effect on the value and must be fully reported in an appraisal. An antique in damaged condition, or lacking the "original brasses," may be worth much less than a similar piece in excellent condition.

Art appraisers. More weight will usually be given to an appraisal prepared by an individual specializing in the kind and price range of the art being appraised. Certain art dealers or appraisers specialize, for example, in old masters, modern art, bronze sculpture, etc. Their opinions on the authenticity and desirability of such art would usually be given more weight than the opinions of more generalized art dealers or appraisers. They can report more recent comparable sales to support their opinion.

To identify and locate experts on unique, specialized items or collections, you may wish to use the current *Official Museum Directory* of the American Association of Museums. It lists museums both by state and by category.

To help you locate a qualified appraiser for your donation, you may wish to ask an art historian at a nearby college or the director or curator of a local museum. The Yellow Pages often list specialized art and antique dealers, auctioneers, and art appraisers. You may also contact associations of dealers for guidance.

Collections

Since many kinds of hobby collections may be the subject of a charitable donation, it is not possible to discuss all of the possible collectibles in this publication. Most common are rare books, autographs, manuscripts, stamps, coins, guns, phonograph records, and natural history items. Many of the elements of valuation that apply to paintings and other objects of art, discussed earlier, also apply to miscellaneous collections.

Reference material. Publications available to help you determine the value of many kinds of collections include catalogs, dealers' price lists, and specialized hobby periodicals. When using one of these price guides, you must use the current edition at the date of contribution. However, these sources are not always reliable indicators of FMV and should be supported by other evidence.

For example, a dealer may sell an item for much less than is shown on a price list, particularly after the item has remained unsold for a long time. The price an item sold for in an auction may have been the result of a rigged sale or a mere bidding duel. The appraiser must analyze the reference material, and recognize and make adjustments for misleading entries. If you are donating a valuable collection, you should get an appraisal. If your donation appears to be of little value, you may be able to make a satisfactory valuation using reference materials available at a state, city, college, or museum library.

Stamp collections. Most libraries have catalogs or other books that report the publisher's estimate of values. Generally, two price levels are shown for each stamp: the price postmarked and the price not postmarked. Stamp dealers generally know the value of their merchandise and are able to prepare satisfactory appraisals of valuable collections.

Coin collections. Many catalogs and other reference materials show the writer's or publisher's opinion of the value of coins on or near the date of the publication. Like many other collectors' items, the value of a coin depends on the demand for it, its age, and its rarity. Another important factor is the coin's condition. For example, there is a great difference in the value of a coin that is in mint condition and a similar coin that is only in good condition.

Catalogs usually establish a category for coins, based on their physical condition—mint or uncirculated, extremely fine, very fine, fine, very good, good, fair, or poor—with a different valuation for each category.

Books. The value of books is usually determined by selecting comparable sales and adjusting the prices according to the differences between the comparable sales and the item being evaluated. This is difficult to do and, except for a collection of little value, should be done by a specialized appraiser. Within the general category of literary property, there are dealers who specialize in certain areas, such as Americana, foreign imports, Bibles, and scientific books.

Modest value of collection. If the collection you are donating is of modest value, not requiring a written appraisal, the following information may help you in determining the FMV.

A book that is very old, or very rare, is not necessarily valuable. There are many books that are very old or rare, but that have little or no market value.

Condition of book. The condition of a book may have a great influence on its value. Collectors are interested in items that are in fine, or at least good, condition. When a book has a missing page, a loose binding, tears, stains, or is otherwise in poor condition, its value is greatly lowered.

Other factors. Some other factors in the valuation of a book are the kind of binding (leather, cloth, paper), page edges, and illustrations (drawings and photographs). Collectors usually want first editions of books. However, because of changes or additions, other editions are sometimes worth as much as, or more than, the first edition.

Manuscripts, autographs, diaries, and similar items. When these items are handwritten, or at least signed by famous people, they are often in demand and are valuable. The writings of unknowns also may be of value if they are of unusual historical or literary importance. Determining the value of such material is difficult. For example, there may be a great difference in value between two diaries that were kept by a famous person—one kept during childhood and the other during a later period in his or her life. The appraiser determines a value in these cases by applying knowledge and judgment to such factors as comparable sales and conditions.

Signatures. Signatures, or sets of signatures, that were cut from letters or other papers usually have little or no value. But complete sets of the signatures of U.S. presidents are in demand.

Cars, Boats, and Aircraft

If you donate a car, a boat, or an aircraft to a charitable organization, its FMV must be determined.

Certain commercial firms and trade organizations publish monthly or seasonal guides for different regions of the country, containing complete dealer sale prices or dealer-average prices for recent model years. Prices are reported for each make, model, and year of used car, aircraft, truck, recreational vehicle, and boat. These guides also provide estimates for adjusting for unusual equipment, unusual mileage, and physical condition. The prices are not "official," and these publications are not considered an appraisal of any specific donated property. But they do provide clues for making an appraisal and suggest relative prices for comparison with current sales and offerings in your area.

These publications are sometimes available at a bank, credit union, or finance company.

Except for inexpensive small boats, the valuation of boats should be based on an appraisal by a marine surveyor because the physical condition is so critical to the value.

  Example. You donate your car to a local high school for use by students studying automobile repair. Your credit union told you that the "blue book" value of a car like yours is $1,600 in good condition. However, your car needs extensive repairs. After checking with repair shops and used car dealers, you find that the car should sell for $750. You may use $750 as the FMV of the car.

Inventory

If you donate any inventory item to a charitable organization, the amount of your deductible contribution is the FMV of the item, less any gain you would have realized if you had sold the item at its FMV on the date of the gift. For more information, see *Charitable contributions* in Chapter 16 of Publication 535, *Business Expenses.*

Stocks and Bonds

The value of stocks and bonds is the FMV of a share or bond on the valuation date. See *Date of contribution,* earlier, under *What Is Fair Market Value (FMV)?*

Selling prices on valuation date. If there is an active market for the con-tributed stocks or bonds on a stock exchange, in an over-the-counter market, or elsewhere, the FMV of each share or bond is the average price between the highest and lowest quoted selling prices on the valuation date. For exam-ple, if the highest selling price for a share was $11, and the lowest $9, the average price is $10. You get the average price by adding $11 and $9 and dividing the sum by 2.

No sales on valuation date. If there were no sales on the valuation date, but there were sales within a reasonable period before and after the valua-tion date, you determine FMV by taking the average price between the high-est and lowest sales prices on the nearest date before and on the nearest date after the valuation date. Then you weight these averages in **inverse** order by the respective number of trading days between the selling dates and the valuation date.

Example. On the day you gave stock to a qualified organization, there were no sales of the stock. Sales of the stock nearest the valuation date took place two trading days before the valuation date at an average selling price of $10 and three trading days after the valuation date at an average selling price of $15. The FMV on the valuation date was $12, figured as follows:

$$[(3 \times \$10) + (2 \times \$15)] \div 5 = \$12$$

Listings on more than one stock exchange. Stocks or bonds listed on more than one stock exchange are valued based on the prices of the exchange on which they are principally dealt. This applies if these prices are published in a generally available listing or publication of general circulation. If this is not applicable, and the stocks or bonds are reported on a composite listing of combined exchanges in a publication of general circulation, use the composite list. See also Unavailable prices or closely held corporation, later.

Bid and asked prices on valuation date. If there were no sales within a reasonable period before and after the valuation date, the FMV is the average price between the bona fide bid and asked prices on the valuation date.

Example. Although there were no sales of Blue Corporation stock on the valuation date, bona fide bid and asked prices were available on that date of $14 and $16, respectively. The FMV is $15, the average price between the bid and asked prices.

No prices on valuation date. If there were no prices available on the valuation date, you determine FMV by taking the average prices between the bona fide bid and asked prices on the closest trading date before and after the valuation date. Both dates must be within a reasonable period. Then you weight these averages in *inverse* order by the respective number of trading days between the bid and asked dates and the valuation date.

Prices only before or after valuation date, but not both. If no selling prices or bona fide bid and asked prices are available on a date within a reasonable period before the valuation date, but are available on a date within a reasonable period after the valuation date, or vice versa, then the average price between the highest and lowest of such available prices may be treated as the value.

Large blocks of stock. When a large block of stock is put on the market, it may lower the selling price of the stock if the supply is greater than the demand. On the other hand, market forces may exist that will afford higher prices for large blocks of stock. Because of the many factors to be considered, determining the value of large blocks of stock usually requires the help of experts specializing in underwriting large quantities of securities, or in trading in the securities of the industry of which the particular company is a part.

Unavailable prices or closely held corporation. If selling prices or bid and asked prices are not available, or if securities of a closely held corporation are involved, determine the FMV by considering the following factors:

1. For bonds, the soundness of the security, the interest yield, the date of maturity, and other relevant factors.
2. For shares of stock, the company's net worth, prospective earning power and dividend-paying capacity, and other relevant factors.

Other factors. Other relevant factors include the goodwill of the business, the economic outlook in the particular industry, the company's position in the industry and its management, and the value of securities of corporations engaged in the same or similar business. For preferred stock, the most important factors are its yield, dividend coverage, and protection of its liquidation preference.

You should keep complete financial and other information on which the valuation is based. This includes copies of reports of examinations of the company made by accountants, engineers, or any technical experts on or close to the valuation date.

Restricted securities. Some classes of stock cannot be traded publicly because of restrictions imposed by the Securities and Exchange Commission, or by the corporate charter or a trust agreement. These restricted securities usually trade at a discount in relation to freely traded securities.

To arrive at the FMV of restricted securities, factors that you must consider include the resale provisions found in the restriction agreements, the relative negotiating strengths of the buyer and seller, and the market experience of freely traded securities of the same class as the restricted securities.

Real Estate

Because each piece of real estate is unique and its valuation is complicated, a detailed appraisal by a professional appraiser is necessary.

The appraiser must be thoroughly trained in the application of appraisal principles and theory. In some instances the opinions of equally qualified appraisers may carry unequal weight, such as when one appraiser has a better knowledge of local conditions.

The appraisal report must contain a complete description of the property, such as street address, legal description, and lot and block number, as well as physical features, condition, and dimensions. The use to which the property is put, zoning and permitted uses, and its potential use for other higher and better uses are also relevant.

In general, there are three main approaches to the valuation of real estate. An appraisal may require the combined use of two or three methods rather than one method only.

1. Comparable Sales

The comparable sales method compares the donated property with several similar properties that have been sold. The selling prices, after adjustments for differences in date of sale, size, condition, and location, would then indicate the estimated FMV of the donated property.

If the comparable sales method is used to determine the value of **unimproved real property** (land without significant buildings, structures, or any other improvements that add to its value), the appraiser should consider the following factors when comparing the potential comparable property and the donated property:

1. Location, size, and zoning or use restrictions,
2. Accessibility and road frontage, and available utilities and water rights,
3. Riparian rights (right of access to and use of the water by owners of land on the bank of a river) and existing easements, rights-of-way, leases, etc.,
4. Soil characteristics, vegetative cover, and status of mineral rights, and
5. Other factors affecting value.

For each comparable sale, the appraisal must include the names of the buyer and seller, the deed book and page number, the date of sale and selling price, a property description, the amount and terms of mortgages, property surveys, the assessed value, the tax rate, and the assessor's appraised FMV.

The comparable selling prices must be adjusted to account for differences between the sale property and the donated property. Because differences of opinion may arise between appraisers as to the degree of comparability and the amount of the adjustment considered necessary for comparison purposes, an appraiser should document each item of adjustment.

Only comparable sales having the least adjustments in terms of items and/or total dollar adjustments should be considered as comparable to the donated property.

2. Capitalization of Income

This method capitalizes the net income from the property at a rate that represents a fair return on the particular investment at the particular time, considering the risks involved. The key elements are the determination of the income to be capitalized and the rate of capitalization.

3. Replacement Cost New or Reproduction
Cost Minus Observed Depreciation

This method, used alone, usually does not result in a determination of FMV. Instead, it generally tends to set the upper limit of value, particularly in periods of rising costs, because it is reasonable to assume that an informed buyer will not pay more for the real estate than it would cost to reproduce a similar property. Of course, this reasoning does not apply if a similar property cannot be created because of location, unusual construction, or some other reason. Generally, this method serves to support the value determined from other methods. When the replacement cost method is applied to **improved realty,** the land and improvements are valued separately.

The replacement cost of a building is figured by considering the materials, the quality of workmanship, and the number of square feet or cubic feet in the building. This cost represents the total cost of labor and material, overhead, and profit. After the replacement cost has been figured, consideration must be given to the following factors:

1. Physical deterioration—the wear and tear on the building itself,

2. Functional obsolescence—usually in older buildings with, for example, inadequate lighting, plumbing, or heating, small rooms, or a poor floor plan, and

3. Economic obsolescence—outside forces causing the whole area to become less desirable.

Interest in a Business

The FMV of any interest in a business, whether a sole proprietorship or a partnership, is the amount that a willing buyer would pay for the interest to a willing seller after consideration of all relevant factors. The relevant factors to be considered in valuing the business are:

1. The FMV of the assets of the business,

2. The demonstrated earnings capacity of the business, based on a review of past and current earnings, and

3. The other factors used in evaluating corporate stock, if they apply.

The value of the goodwill of the business should also be taken into consideration. You should keep complete financial and other information on which you base the valuation. This includes copies of reports of examinations of the business made by accountants, engineers, or any technical experts on or close to the valuation date.

Annuities, Interests for Life or Terms of Years, Remainders, and Reversions

The value of these kinds of property is their present value, except in the case of annuities under contracts issued by companies regularly engaged in their sale. The valuation of these commercial annuity contracts and of insurance policies is discussed later under *Certain Life Insurance and Annuity Contracts*.

To determine present value, you must know the applicable interest rate and use actuarial tables.

Interest rate. The applicable interest rate varies. It is announced monthly in a news release and published in the Internal Revenue Bulletin as a Revenue Ruling. The interest rate to use is under the heading "Rate Under Section 7520" for a given month and year. You can call the local IRS office to obtain this rate.

Actuarial tables. You need to refer to actuarial tables to determine a qualified interest in the form of an annuity, any interest for life or a term of years, or any remainder interest to a charitable organization.

Use the valuation tables set forth in IRS Publications 1457 (Alpha Volume) and 1458 (Beta Volume). Both of these publications provide tables containing actuarial factors to be used in determining the present value of an annuity, an interest for life or for a term of years, or a remainder or reversionary interest. For qualified charitable transfers, you can use the factor for the month in which you made the contribution or for either of the 2 months preceding that month.

Publication 1457 also contains actuarial factors for computing the value of a remainder interest in a charitable remainder annuity trust and a pooled income fund. Publication 1458 contains the factors for valuing the remainder interest in a charitable remainder unitrust. These are available for purchase by phone at (202) 512-1800 or by mail from the:

> Superintendent of Documents
> United States Government
> Printing Office
> P.O. Box 371954
> Pittsburgh, PA 15250-7954

If you call in your order, you can pay by VISA or MasterCard.

Tables containing actuarial factors for transfers to pooled income funds may also be found in Income Tax Regulation 1.642(c)-6(e)(5), transfers to charitable remainder unitrusts in Regulation 1.664(e)(6), and other transfers in Regulation 20.2031-7(d)(6).

Special factors. If you need a special factor for an actual transaction, you may ask for it by writing a request for a letter ruling to the:

> Internal Revenue Service
> Associate Chief Counsel (Domestic)
> Attn: CC:DOM:Corp:T
> P.O. Box 7604
> Ben Franklin Station
> Washington, DC 20044

Be sure to include the date of birth of each person, the duration of whose life may affect the value of the interest, and copies of the relevant instruments. IRS charges a user fee for providing special factors.

For information on the circumstances under which a charitable deduction may be allowed for the donation of a partial interest in property not in trust, see *Partial Interest in Property Not in Trust*, later.

Certain Life Insurance and Annuity Contracts

The value of an annuity contract or a life insurance policy issued by a company regularly engaged in the sale of such contracts or policies is the amount that company would charge for a comparable contract.

But if the donee of a life insurance policy may reasonably be expected to cash the policy rather than hold it as an investment, then the FMV is the cash surrender value rather than the replacement cost.

If an annuity is payable under a combination annuity contract and life insurance policy (for example, a retirement income policy with a death benefit) and there was no insurance element when it was transferred to the charity, the policy is treated as an annuity contract.

Partial Interest in Property Not in Trust

Generally, no deduction is allowed for a charitable contribution, not made in trust, of less than your entire interest in property. However, this does not apply to a transfer of less than your entire interest if it is a transfer of:

1. A remainder interest in your personal residence or farm,
2. An undivided part of your entire interest in property, or
3. A qualified conservation contribution.

Valuation of a remainder interest in real property, not transferred in trust. The amount of the deduction for a donation of a remainder interest in real property is the FMV of the remainder interest at the time of the contribution. To determine this value, you must know the FMV of the property on the date of the contribution. Multiply this value by the appropriate factor. Publications 1457 and 1458 contain these factors.

You must make an adjustment for depreciation or depletion using the factors shown in Publication 1459 (Gamma Volume). You can use the factors for the month in which you made the contribution or for either of the two months preceding that month. See the earlier discussion on *Annuities, Interests for Life or Terms of Years, Remainders, and Reversions.* Publication 1459 is available free by writing to the IRS address given under *Special factors* earlier.

For this purpose, the term "depreciable property" means any property subject to wear and tear or obsolescence, even if not used in a trade or business or for the production of income.

If the remainder interest includes both depreciable and nondepreciable property, for example a house and land, the FMV must be allocated between each kind of property at the time of the contribution. This rule also applies to a gift of a remainder interest that includes property that is part depletable and part not depletable. Take into account depreciation or depletion only for the property that is subject to depreciation or depletion.

For more information, see section 1.170A-2 of the Income Tax Regulations.

Undivided part of your entire interest. A contribution of an undivided part of your entire interest in property must consist of a part of each and every substantial interest or right you own in the property. It must extend over the entire term of your interest in the property. For example, you are entitled to the income from certain property for your life (life estate) and you contribute 20% of that life estate to a qualified organization. You can claim a deduction for the contribution if you do not have any other interest in the property. To figure the value of a contribution involving a partial interest, see Publication 1457.

If the only interest you own in real property is a remainder interest and you transfer part of that interest to a qualified organization, see the previous discussion on valuation of a remainder interest in real property.

Qualified conservation contribution. A qualified conservation contribution is a contribution of a qualified real property interest to a qualified organization to be used only for conservation purposes.

Qualified organization. For purposes of a qualified conservation contribution, a qualified organization is:

1. A governmental unit,
2. A publicly supported charitable, religious, scientific, literary, educational, etc., organization, or
3. An organization that is controlled by, and operated for the exclusive benefit of, a governmental unit or a publicly supported charity.

Conservation purposes. Your contribution must be made only for one of the following conservation purposes:

1. Preservation of land areas for outdoor recreation by, or for the education of, the general public.
2. Protection of a relatively natural habitat of fish, wildlife, or plants, or a similar ecosystem.
3. Preservation of open space, including farmland and forest land. The preservation must yield a significant public benefit. It must be either for the scenic enjoyment of the general public or under a clearly defined federal, state, or local governmental conservation policy.
4. Preservation of a historically important land area or a certified historic structure. A historically important land area includes an independently significant land area, any land area in a registered historic district, and any land area next to a property listed in the National Register of Historic Places if its physical or environmental features contribute to the historic or cultural integrity of the listed property. A certified historic structure is any building, structure, or land area that is listed in the National Register, or is located in a registered historic district and is certified by the Secretary of the Interior as being of historic significance to the district.

There must be some visual public access to the property. Factors used in determining the type and amount of public access required include the historical significance of the property, the remoteness or accessibility of the site, and the extent to which intrusions of privacy would be unreasonable.

Qualified real property interest. This is any of the following interests in real property:

1. Your entire interest in real estate other than a mineral interest (subsurface oil, gas, or other minerals, and the right of access to these minerals).

2 A remainder interest.

3. A restriction (granted in perpetuity) on the use which may be made of the real property.

Valuation. A qualified real property interest described in 1 should be valued in a manner that is consistent with the type of interest transferred. If you transferred all the interest in the property, the FMV of the property is the amount of the contribution. If you do not transfer the mineral interest, the FMV of the surface rights in the property is the amount of the contribution.

If you owned only a remainder interest or an income interest (life estate), see *Undivided part of your entire interest,* earlier. If you owned the entire property but only transferred a remainder interest (item 2), see *Valuation of a remainder interest in real property, not transferred in trust,* earlier.

In determining the value of restrictions, you should take into account the selling price in arm's-length transactions of other properties that have comparable restrictions. If there are no qualified sales, the restrictions are valued indirectly as the difference between the FMVs of the property involved before and after the grant of the restriction.

The FMV of the property before contribution of the restriction should take into account not only current use but the likelihood that the property, without the restriction, would be developed. You should also consider any zoning, conservation, or historical preservation laws that would restrict development. Granting an easement may increase, rather than reduce, the value of property, and in such a situation no deduction would be allowed.

Example. You own 10 acres of farmland. Similar land in the area has an FMV of $2,000 an acre. However, land in the general area that is restricted

solely to farm use has an FMV of $1,500 an acre. Your county wants to pre-
serve open space and prevent further development in your area.

You grant to the county an enforceable open space easement in perpetuity
on 8 of the 10 acres, restricting its use to farmland. The value of this easement is $4,000, determined as follows:

> *FMV of the property before granting easement:*
> *$2,000 × 10 acres* $20,000
>
> *FMV of the property after granting easement:*
> *$1,500 × 8 acres* $12,000
> *$2,000 × 2 acres*   4,000   16,000
>
> *Value of easement* $4,000

If you later transfer in fee your remaining interest in the 8 acres to another
qualified organization, the FMV of your remaining interest is the FMV of
the 8 acres reduced by the FMV of the easement granted to the first
organization.

Appraisals

Appraisals are not necessary for items of property for which you claim a
deduction of $5,000 or less, or for which the value can easily be deter-
mined, such as securities whose prices are reported daily in the newspapers.
However, you generally will need an appraisal for donated property for
which you claim a deduction of more than $5,000. See *Deductions of More
Than $5,000,* later.

The weight given an appraisal depends on the completeness of the report,
the qualifications of the appraiser, and the appraiser's demonstrated knowledge of the donated property. An appraisal must give all the facts on which
to base an intelligent judgment of the value of the property.

The appraisal will not be given much weight if:
1. All the factors that apply are not considered,
2. The opinion is not supported with facts, such as purchase price and
   comparable sales, or
3. The opinion is not consistent with known facts.

The appraiser's opinion is never more valid than the facts on which it is based; without these facts it is simply a guess.

Membership in professional appraisal or dealer organizations does not automatically establish the appraiser's competency. Nor does the lack of certificates, memberships, etc., automatically disprove the competency of the appraiser.

The opinion of a person claiming to be an expert is not binding on the Internal Revenue Service. All facts associated with the donation must be considered.

Cost of appraisals. You may not take a charitable contribution deduction for fees you pay for appraisals of your donated property. However, these fees may qualify as a miscellaneous deduction, subject to the 2% limit, on Schedule A (Form 1040) if paid to determine the amount allowable as a charitable contribution.

Deductions of More Than $5,000

Generally, if the claimed deduction for an item or group of similar items of donated property is more than $5,000, other than money and publicly traded securities, you must get a qualified appraisal made by a qualified appraiser, and you must attach an appraisal summary (Section B of Form 8283) to your tax return. You should keep the appraiser's report with your written records. Records are discussed in Publication 526. For special rules that apply to publicly traded securities and nonpublicly traded stock, see the discussions later in this section.

The phrase **similar items** means property of the same generic category or type (whether or not donated to the same donee), such as stamps, coins, lithographs, paintings, photographs, books, nonpublicly traded stock, nonpublicly traded securities other than nonpublicly traded stock, land, buildings, clothing, jewelry, furniture, electronic equipment, household appliances, toys, everyday kitchenware, china, crystal, or silver. For example, if you give books to three schools and you deduct $2,000, $2,500, and $900, respectively, your claimed deduction is more than $5,000 for these books. You must get a qualified appraisal of the books and for each school you must attach a fully completed appraisal summary (Section B of Form 8283) to your tax return.

Publicly traded securities. Even if your claimed deduction is more than $5,000, neither a qualified appraisal nor an appraisal summary is required for publicly traded securities that are:

- Listed on a stock exchange in which quotations are published on a daily basis,
- Regularly traded in a national or regional over-the-counter market for which published quotations are available, or
- Shares of an open-end investment company (mutual fund) for which quotations are published on a daily basis in a newspaper of general circulation throughout the United States.

Publicly traded securities that meet these requirements must be reported in Section A, Form 8283.

A partially completed appraisal summary (Parts I and IV of Section B, Form 8283) signed by the donee, but not a qualified appraisal, is required for publicly traded securities that do not meet these requirements, but do have readily available market quotations. Market quotations are readily available if:

1. The issue is regularly traded during the computation period (defined later) in a market for which there is an "interdealer quotation system" (defined later),

2. The issuer or agent computes the "average trading price" (defined later) for the same issue for the computation period,

3. The average trading price and total volume of the issue during the computation period are published in a newspaper of general circulation throughout the United States, not later than the last day of the month following the end of the calendar quarter in which the computation period ends,

4. The issuer or agent keeps books and records that list for each transaction during the computation period the date of settlement of the transaction, the name and address of the broker or dealer making the market in which the transaction occurred, and the trading price and volume, and

5. The issuer or agent permits the Internal Revenue Service to review the books and records described in paragraph (4) with respect to transactions during the computation period upon receiving reasonable notice.

An **interdealer quotation system** is any system of general circulation to brokers and dealers that regularly disseminates quotations of obligations by two or more identified brokers or dealers who are not related to either the issuer or agent who computes the average trading price of the security. A quotation sheet prepared and distributed by a broker or dealer in the regular course of business and containing only quotations of that broker or dealer is not an interdealer quotation system.

The **average trading price** is the average price of all transactions (weighted by volume), other than original issue or redemption transactions, conducted through a United States office of a broker or dealer who maintains a market in the issue of the security during the computation period. Bid and asked quotations are not taken into account.

The **computation period** is weekly during October through December and monthly during January through September. The weekly computation periods during October through December begin with the first Monday in October and end with the first Sunday following the last Monday in December.

Nonpublicly traded stock. If you contribute nonpublicly traded stock, for which you claim a deduction of $10,000 or less, a qualified appraisal is not required. However, you must attach to your tax return a partially completed appraisal summary (Parts I and IV of Section B, Form 8283) signed by the donee.

Qualified Appraisal

Generally, if the claimed deduction for an item or group of similar items of donated property is more than $5,000, you must get a qualified appraisal made by a qualified appraiser and you must attach an appraisal summary to your tax return. See *Deductions of More Than $5,000*, earlier.

A qualified appraisal is an appraisal document that:

1. Relates to an appraisal made not earlier than 60 days prior to the date of contribution of the appraised property,
2. Does not involve a prohibited appraisal fee,
3. Includes certain information (covered later), and
4. Is prepared, signed, and dated by a qualified appraiser (defined later).

You must receive the qualified appraisal before the due date, including extensions, of the return on which a charitable contribution deduction is first claimed for the donated property. If the deduction is first claimed on an amended return, the qualified appraisal must be received before the date on which the amended return is filed.

An appraisal summary (discussed later) must be attached to your tax return. Generally, you do not need to attach the qualified appraisal itself, but you should keep a copy as long as it may be relevant under the tax law. If you donated art valued at $20,000 or more, however, you must attach a complete copy of the signed appraisal. See *Paintings, Antiques, and Other Objects of Art*, discussed earlier under *Valuation of Various Kinds of Property*.

Prohibited appraisal fee. Generally, no part of the fee arrangement for a qualified appraisal can be based on a percentage of the appraised value of the property. If a fee arrangement is based on what is allowed as a deduction, after Internal Revenue Service examination or otherwise, it is treated as a fee based on a percentage of appraised value. However, appraisals are not disqualified when an otherwise prohibited fee is paid to a generally recognized association that regulates appraisers if:

- The association is not organized for profit and no part of its net earnings benefits any private shareholder or individual,
- The appraiser does not receive any compensation from the association or any other persons for making the appraisal, and
- The fee arrangement is not based in whole or in part on the amount of the appraised value that is allowed as a deduction after an Internal Revenue Service examination or otherwise.

Information included in qualified appraisal. A qualified appraisal must include the following information:

1. A description of the property in sufficient detail for a person who is not generally familiar with the type of property to determine that the property appraised is the property that was (or will be) contributed,
2. The physical condition of any tangible property,
3. The date (or expected date) of contribution,
4. The terms of any agreement or understanding entered into (or expected to be entered into) by or on behalf of the donor that relates to the use, sale, or other disposition of the donated property,
5. The name, address, and taxpayer identification number of the qualified appraiser and, if the appraiser is a partner, an employee, or an independent contractor engaged by a person other than the donor, the name, address, and taxpayer identification number of the partnership or the person who employs or engages the appraiser,

6. The qualifications of the qualified appraiser who signs the appraisal, including the appraiser's background, experience, education, and any membership in professional appraisal associations,

7. A statement that the appraisal was prepared for income tax purposes,

8. The date (or dates) on which the property was valued,

9. The appraised FMV on the date (or expected date) of contribution,

10. The method of valuation used to determine FMV, such as the income approach, the comparable sales or market data approach, or the replacement cost less depreciation approach, and

11. The specific basis for the valuation, such as any specific comparable sales transaction.

Art objects. The following are examples of information that should be included in a description of donated property. These examples are for art objects. A similar detailed breakdown should be given for other property. Appraisals of art objects—paintings in particular—should include:

1. A complete description of the object, indicating the:

    a. Size,

    b. Subject matter,

    c. Medium,

    d. Name of the artist (or culture), and

    e. Approximate date created.

2. The cost, date, and manner of acquisition.

3. A history of the item, including proof of authenticity.

4. A photograph of a size and quality fully showing the object, preferably a 10 × 12 inch print.

5. The facts on which the appraisal was based, such as:

    a. Sales or analyses of similar works by the artist, particularly on or around the valuation date.

    b. Quoted prices in dealer's catalogs of the artist's works or works of other artists of comparable stature.

    c. A record of any exhibitions at which the specific art object had been displayed.

    d. The economic state of the art market at the time of valuation, particularly with respect to the specific property.

    e. The standing of the artist in his profession and in the particular school or time period.

Number of qualified appraisals. A separate qualified appraisal is required for each item of property that is not included in a group of similar items of property. You need only one qualified appraisal for a group of similar items of property contributed in the same tax year, but you may get separate appraisals for each item. A qualified appraisal for a group of similar items must provide all of the required information for each item of similar property. The appraiser, however, may provide a group description for selected items, the total value of which is not more than $100.

Qualified appraiser. A qualified appraiser is an individual who declares on the appraisal summary that he or she:

- Holds himself or herself out to the public as an appraiser or performs appraisals on a regular basis,
- Is qualified to make appraisals of the type of property being valued because of his or her qualifications described in the appraisal,
- Is not an excluded individual, and
- Understands that an intentionally false overstatement of the value of property may subject him or her to the penalty for aiding and abetting an understatement of tax liability.

An appraiser must complete Part III of Section B (Form 8283) to be considered a qualified appraiser. More than one appraiser may appraise the property, provided that each complies with the requirements, including signing the qualified appraisal and appraisal summary.

Excluded individuals. The following persons cannot be qualified appraisers with respect to particular property:

1. The donor of the property, or the taxpayer who claims the deduction.
2. The donee of the property.
3. A party to the transaction in which the donor acquired the property being appraised, unless the property is donated within 2 months of the date of acquisition and its appraised value does not exceed its acquisition price. This applies to the person who sold, exchanged, or gave the property to the donor, or any person who acted as an agent for the transferor or donor in the transaction.
4. Any person employed by, married to, or related under section 267(b) of the Internal Revenue Code, to any of the above persons. For example, if the donor acquired a painting from an art dealer, neither the dealer nor persons employed by the dealer can be qualified appraisers for that painting.

5. An appraiser who appraises regularly for a person in 1, 2, or 3, and who does not perform a majority of his or her appraisals made during his or her tax year for other persons.

In addition, a person is not a qualified appraiser for a particular donation if the donor had knowledge of facts that would cause a reasonable person to expect the appraiser to falsely overstate the value of the donated property. For example, if the donor and the appraiser make an agreement concerning the amount at which the property will be valued, and the donor knows that such amount exceeds the FMV of the property, the appraiser is not a qualified appraiser for the donation.

Penalties. Any appraiser who falsely or fraudulently overstates the value of property described in a qualified appraisal or an appraisal summary that the appraiser has signed may be subject to a civil penalty for aiding and abetting an understatement of tax liability, and may have his or her appraisal disregarded.

Appraisal Summary

Generally, if the claimed deduction for an item of donated property is more than $5,000, you must attach an appraisal summary (Form 8283) to your tax return. Only a partially completed appraisal summary is required in some situations. See *Deductions of More Than $5,000,* earlier.

Note: If you deduct $20,000 or more for donated art, you must attach a complete copy of the signed appraisal. See *Paintings, Antiques, and Other Objects of Art,* discussed earlier under *Valuation of Various Kinds of Property.*

Form 8283. Section B of Form 8283 is the appraisal summary. If you do not attach the form to your return, the deduction will not be allowed unless your failure to attach it was due to a good faith omission. If the IRS requests that you submit the form because you did not attach it to your return, you must comply within 90 days of the request or the deduction will be disallowed.

You must attach a separate Form 8283 for each item of contributed property that is not part of a group of similar items. If you contribute similar items of property to the same donee organization, you need attach only one Form 8283 for those items. If you contribute similar items of property to more than one donee organization, you must attach a separate form for each donee.

Internal Revenue Service Review of Appraisals

In reviewing an income tax return, the Service may accept the claimed value of the donated property, based on information or appraisals sent with the return, or may make its own determination of FMV. In either case, the Service may:

- Contact the taxpayer to get more information,
- Refer the valuation problem to a Service appraiser or valuation specialist,
- Refer the issue to the Commissioner's Art Advisory Panel (a 25-member group of dealers and museum directors who review and recommend acceptance or adjustment of taxpayers' claimed values for major paintings and sculptures, Far Eastern and Asian art, Primitive and Pre-Columbian art), or
- Contract with an independent dealer, scholar, or appraiser to appraise the property when the objects require appraisers of highly specialized experience and knowledge.

Responsibility of the Service. The Service is responsible for reviewing appraisals, but it is not responsible for making them. Supporting the FMV listed on your return is your responsibility.

The Service does not accept appraisals without question. Nor does the Service recognize any particular appraiser or organization of appraisers.

Timing of Service action. The Service generally does not approve valuations or appraisals before the actual filing of the tax return to which the appraisal applies. In addition, the Service generally does not issue advance rulings approving or disapproving such appraisals.

   Exception. On January 16, 1996, the Service began accepting requests for a **Statement of Value** for a donated item of art appraised at $50,000 or more. For a request submitted as described earlier under *Art valued at $50,000 or more*, the Service will issue a Statement of Value that can be relied on by the donor of the item of art.

Penalties

You may be liable for a penalty if you overstate the value or adjusted basis of donated property.

20% penalty. The penalty is 20% of the underpayment of tax related to the overstatement if:

1. The value or adjusted basis claimed on the return is 200% or more of the correct amount, and

2. You underpaid your tax by more than $5,000 because of the overstatement.

40% penalty. The penalty is 40%, rather than 20%, if:

1. The value or adjusted basis claimed on the return is 400% or more of the correct amount, and

2. You underpaid your tax by more than $5,000 because of the overstatement.

How to Get More Information

You can order free publications and forms, ask tax questions, and get more information from the IRS in several ways. By selecting the method that is best for you, you will have quick and easy access to tax help.

Free tax services. To find out what services are available, get Publication 910, *Guide to Free Tax Services*. It contains a list of free tax publications and an index of tax topics. It also describes other free tax information services, including tax education and assistance programs and a list of TeleTax topics.

Personal computer. With your personal computer and modem, you can access the IRS on the Internet at **www.irs.gov**. While visiting our web site, you can select:

*   *Frequently Asked Tax Questions* (located under *Taxpayer Help & Ed*) to find answers to questions you may have.
*   *Forms & Pubs* to download forms and publications or search for forms and publications by topic or keyword.
*   *Fill-in Forms* (located under *Forms & Pubs*) to enter information while the form is displayed and then print the completed form.
*   *Tax Info For You* to view Internal Revenue Bulletins published in the last few years.
*   *Tax Regs in English* to search regulations and the Internal Revenue Code (under *United States Code (USC)*).
*   *Digital Dispatch* and *IRS Local News Net* (both located under *Tax Info For Business*) to receive our electronic newsletters on hot tax issues and news.

- *Small Business Corner* (located under *Tax Info For Business*) to get information on starting and operating a small business.

You can also reach us with your computer using File Transfer Protocol at **ftp.irs.gov.**

TaxFax Service: Using the phone attached to your fax machine, you can receive forms and instructions by calling **703-368-9694.** Follow the directions from the prompts. When you order forms, enter the catalog number for the form you need. The items you request will be faxed to you.

Phone: Many services are available by phone.

- *Ordering forms, instructions, and publications.* Call **1-800-829-3676** to order current and prior year forms, instructions, and publications.
- *Asking tax questions.* Call the IRS with your tax questions at **1-800-829-1040.**
- *TTY/TDD equipment.* If you have access to TTY/TDD equipment, call **1-800-829-4059** to ask tax questions or to order forms and publications.
- *TeleTax topics.* Call **1-800-829-4477** to listen to pre-recorded messages covering various tax topics.

   Evaluating the quality of our telephone services. To ensure that IRS representatives give accurate, courteous, and professional answers, we evaluate the quality of our telephone services in several ways.

- A second IRS representative sometimes monitors live telephone calls. That person only evaluates the IRS assistor and does not keep a record of any taxpayer's name or tax identification number.
- We sometimes record telephone calls to evaluate IRS assistors objectively. We hold these recordings no longer than one week and use them only to measure the quality of assistance.
- We value our customers' opinions. Throughout this year, we will be surveying our customers for their opinions on our service.

Walk-in: You can walk in to many post offices, libraries, and IRS offices to pick up certain forms, instructions, and publications. Also, some libraries and IRS offices have:

- An extensive collection of products available to print from a CD-ROM or photocopy from reproducible proofs.
- The Internal Revenue Code, regulations, Internal Revenue Bulletins, and Cumulative Bulletins available for research purposes.

Mail: You can send your order for forms, instructions, and publications to the Distribution Center nearest to you and receive a response within 10 workdays after your request is received. Find the address that applies to your part of the country.

- Western part of United States:
  Western Area Distribution Center
  Rancho Cordova, CA 95743-0001

- Central part of United States:
  Central Area Distribution Center
  P.O. Box 8903
  Bloomington, IL 61702-8903

- Eastern part of United States and foreign addresses:
  Eastern Area Distribution Center
  P.O. Box 85074
  Richmond, VA 23261-5074

CD-ROM: You can order IRS Publication 1796, *Federal Tax Products on CD-ROM*, and obtain:

- Current tax forms, instructions, and publications.

- Prior-year tax forms, instructions, and publications.

- Popular tax forms which may be filled in electronically, printed out for submission, and saved for recordkeeping.

- Internal Revenue Bulletins.

The CD-ROM can be purchased from National Technical Information Service (NTIS) by calling **1-877-233-6767** or on the Internet at **www.irs.gov/cdorders**. The first release is available in mid-December and the final release is available in late January.

IRS Publication 3207, *Small Business Resource Guide*, is an interactive CD-ROM that contains information important to small businesses. It is available in mid-February. You can get one free copy by calling **1-800-829-3676.**

PricewaterhouseCoopers' Personal Financial Services

About PricewaterhouseCoopers Personal Financial Services

PricewaterhouseCoopers' Personal Financial Services practice provides comprehensive financial planning services designed to help build, preserve, and maximize the wealth of high net worth individuals, corporate executives, and business owners. We work with these individuals to develop integrated financial strategies that consider the numerous aspects of wealth accumulation and its ramifications on their business and family.

PricewaterhouseCoopers' assets in the area of personal financial services include the talents of more than 400 full-time financial planning advisers in the United States and another 200 advisers in locations throughout the world. With extensive experience and knowledge, we bring a broad perspective to assessing and planning wealth goals.

Personal Financial Services Partner Resources

Central Region

Illinois

Chicago	Larry D. Brown	312-298-2214

Michigan

Detroit	Bernard S. Kent	313-394-6537

Missouri

St. Louis	Rebecca S. Weaver	314-206-8490

Ohio

Cleveland	Brian K. Gothot	216-875-3456

Texas

Dallas	Kevin F. Roach	214-754-7261
Houston	Bruce J. Belman	713-356-4680

New York Metro Region

New Jersey

Florham Park	Steven A. Calvelli	973-236-5595

New York

New York	Vincent D. Vaccaro	646-394-2545
New York	Kent E. Allison	646-394-4259
New York	Evelyn M. Capassakis	646-394-2363

Northeast Region

Massachusetts

Boston	Richard L. Kohan	617-439-7461
Boston	Mark J. Bonner	617-428-8140
Boston	Douglas A. Theobald	617-439-7444

Southeast Region

District of Columbia

Washington D.C.	Arnold H. Koonin	202-414-1049

Florida

Miami	Allison P. Shipley	305-375-6303
Miami	Richard S. Wagman	305-381-7650

Georgia

Atlanta	Bernard E. Palmer	678-419-7335

North Carolina

Charlotte	Robert D. Lyerly	704-344-7521

Pennsylvania

Philadelphia	Michael B. Kennedy	267-330-6075
	Karl T. Weger	267-330-2496

West Region

California

Los Angeles	David D. Green	213-236-3329
San Francisco	Dennis G. Whipp	415-498-7995
	Alfred A. Peguero	415-498-7830
	Scott A. Torgan	415-498-7955

Index